MISSION AL JAZEERA

BUILD A BRIDGE
SEEK THE TRUTH
CHANGE THE WORLD

MISSION AL JAZEERA

JOSH RUSHING

IN COLLABORATION WITH
SEAN ELDER

palgrave
macmillan

MISSION AL JAZEERA
Copyright © Josh Rushing, 2007.
All rights reserved. No part of this book may be used or reproduced in any
manner whatsoever without written permission except in the case of brief
quotations embodied in critical articles or reviews.

First published in 2007 by
PALGRAVE MACMILLAN™
175 Fifth Avenue, New York, N.Y. 10010 and
Houndmills, Basingstoke, Hampshire, England RG21 6XS.
Companies and representatives throughout the world.

PALGRAVE MACMILLAN is the global academic imprint of the
Palgrave Macmillan division of St. Martin's Press, LLC and of Palgrave
Macmillan Ltd. Macmillan® is a registered trademark in the United States,
United Kingdom and other countries. Palgrave is a registered trademark in
the European Union and other countries.

ISBN–13: 978–1–4039–7905–6
ISBN–10: 1–4039–7905–7

Cataloging-in-Publication Data is available from the Library of Congress.

A catalogue record of the book is available from the British Library.

Design by Letra Libre, Inc.

First edition: June 2007

10 9 8 7 6 5 4 3 2 1

Printed in the United States of America.

*To all who fight for the freedoms and principles
for which America should always stand*

and

to Paige, of course.

CONTENTS

ACKNOWLEDGMENTS

I'm deeply indebted to many for the completion of this book. Sean Elder, with great insight, effort and patience, gave structure and shape to my stories and made writing this book possible. Alessandra Bastagli weathered the storm of my personal chaos with a resilience and determination rare in any profession, but essential as my editor.

Luke Janklow, my agent and trusted advisor, keeps a constant vigil on my integrity and credibility in his endless efforts on my behalf.

Lawrence Pintak, Adel Iskander and Marc Lynch helped Sean and me better understand and explain Al Jazeera's importance in the context of Arab media.

Paul Gibbs, a true maverick, recognized a potential in and took a chance on me. Jehane Noujaim shared me with the world in a thoughtful and sensitive way.

Gippy and Gayle Lowery, my in-laws, always understood my absence during visits and holidays while I was writing.

My parents, Gayland and Dinah Rushing, have always loved and supported me, even when, and indeed especially when, I made it difficult. D'Lee Reagh, my first teacher who tirelessly read to me when I was young, was the best big sister anyone could ask for. Sammie Mae and Glenn Edward Bailey—better known to 80-plus grandchildren as Grandma and Grandpa—taught me to love books, challenge the accepted and live my life unfettered by the judgments of others.

Most of all, I'm thankful for my family. My sons, Joshua Luke and Ethan Coltrane, endured fatherless nights and weekends while I wrote this book. May you each find your own missions and be surrounded by the kind of support with which I have been blessed. And I owe everything, everything, everything to my wife Paige who has given me more support and understanding than I deserve or will ever be able to fully return. Paige has been my spouse and friend; caretaker of my children; manager of my home and personal affairs; as well as my most critical editor and even occasional writer in absentia. On every all-nighter it took to complete this book, I was never alone; Paige stayed awake and saw it through even when I failed to. Without Paige, this book would not exist, and even more importantly, I would not be who I am today. Thank you.

INTRODUCTION
MISSION AL JAZEERA

In Arabic the word *jihad* means struggle, or holy war. Many Islamic scholars distinguish between what they call the greater and lesser jihads: the lesser is the fight to defend the faith; the greater is the struggle to overcome the chasm between the best and worst within oneself.

Since the terrorist attacks of September 11, 2001, America has been engaged in its own jihads, both the lesser and the greater. With troops deployed around the world presumably defending their homeland (while offending nearly everyone else), one might call it a victory in this lesser jihad that at the time of this writing there have been no new attacks on the United States since the Twin Towers fell. However, reports from the frontlines of America's greater jihad—the struggle for the nation's soul, the ideas America is supposed to represent—are much more grim.

For fourteen years as a U.S. Marine I dedicated my life to defending America, but through a surprising series of events I have found myself pulled from the fight against foreign enemies and thrown onto the frontlines of America's greater jihad, as a correspondent for Al Jazeera English.

I have an office four floors above our studio in a building three blocks from the White House in Washington, D.C. From this vantage point, in the heart of our nation's capital, I often find myself traversing the battle lines of America's struggle with the best and worst of itself. Such was the case when I went to shoot a story on America's dwindling rural population in Small (and getting smaller) Town, USA.

In a country consumed with immigration issues, I wanted to explore a corner obsessed with emigration. Producer Peggy Holter, cameraman Mark Teboe, and I headed to Divide County (population 2,200), in rural northwest North Dakota, just a few miles south of the Canadian border. There I interviewed everyone, from high school students to business owners, about the value of their little piece of the heartland and the risk of it emptying out as young people went away to college and found little reason to return home afterward. I first sensed something might be amiss when a reporter from *The Journal*, the local paper, showed up to cover me covering them on my first day in the area. She was friendly enough, but after chatting for a bit she admitted to her surprise about how I was dressed. I thought blue jeans and a khaki shirt might appear more causal than what she was accustomed to seeing reporters wear on television.

"No," she said, "it's just that when I heard there was a crew here from Al Jazeera I thought you'd be wearing robes and headscarves."

Although this wouldn't have been true even if I had been working for Al Jazeera Arabic—the original Al Jazeera—I took the opportunity to tell her about Al Jazeera English, which at the time was preparing its global launch, and the story on "vanishing America" that we were pursuing in her neck of the woods. She seemed fine with my explanation, we parted amicably, and I didn't give it much further thought until she called me a few days later, sounding more than a little distraught.

She told me that a couple of days after we met, a man who identified himself as an agent from Customs and Border Protection entered her office and asked her to step outside with him. She asked if she could bring her reporter's notebook, to which he sternly replied, "No need. I'll be the one asking the questions." Once out of the office he began to grill her about her encounter with me: Did he look American? Do you think he was a citizen? What kinds of questions did he ask? What were they doing up here near the border? Did they take pictures or videos? The agent informed her there were potential international implications to my visit, on which he was not at liberty to elaborate.

This impromptu interrogation left her upset, and, since headlines at the time were exposing (and criticizing) the U.S. intelligence services for maintaining a list of private phone numbers they sometimes tapped in search of potential terrorists, she also worried about having been added to that database. Would calling her mother to discuss the interrogation put her on the list as well? She e-mailed her brother in Washington State, who, like his sister, found the story alarming, and hesitated before calling to reassure her. When he hung up the phone, he saw an unmarked car pull up in front of his house. A man leaned out of the passenger side, spray-painted a strange symbol on the sidewalk in front of the house and drove off.

He was dumbfounded by what he saw, and had he not taken a picture of it, even his sister may not have believed him. Overcoming her fear, she wrote a column about her bizarre encounter in *The Journal*, while her brother recounted his own version of the story on his blog. The fuse was ignited: from there, a watchdog group that wrongfully associates Al Jazeera with Al Qaeda picked up the story and released an urgent media advisory about Al Jazeera probing the United States's unsecured borders. This story gained national exposure when Fox News ran a note about it on its ticker. A legion of conservative bloggers propelled the incident even further, fanning the flames of their xenophobic followers with visions of Arabs teeming at the United States's porous border with Canada.

Back in North Dakota, the Customs and Border Protection agent who had visited the reporter was now tracing my footsteps, giving the same big-brother treatment to everyone I interviewed, prompting a series of nervous phone calls to me. They were worried they might have said something that could put their country at risk or, even scarier, something that could have put themselves at risk from their own country. The agent effectively burned every bridge I had crossed in North Dakota, ensuring that there weren't going to be any follow-up interviews on this story.

All of this might have been more amusing than frustrating, were it not for a bolt of bad news I received the same day I found out about the federal agent following me. In an e-mail from an old friend, I learned that one of my best friends from high school, Matthew Worrell, had just been killed in Iraq when his Little Bird helicopter was shot down in a battle south of Baghdad. Like me, Matt had two sons who looked just like him. Jake was three years old and Luke, which is my son's name as well, was eighteen months old. Matt's death hit me hard. At the funeral, his sons wore tiny suits and Luke sucked on a pacifier with a red, white, and blue handle that matched the colors of the flag draped over his father's coffin.

Matt's death reminded me that the struggle, the lesser jihad the United States currently faces, comes at a high cost.

What angered me most was that Matt died serving an idea of America—the idea of a nation with an open mind and heart—that resembled the actual state of America less and less, and seemed to be vanishing faster than the people in North Dakota.

The nation was becoming one blinded by fear, seeing enemies where there weren't any, and treating honest inquiry—the kind guaranteed in the Constitution—with suspicion or hostility.

I called the agent who was on my trail, and this time the questions were for him. Why was he harassing the people I interviewed? If he had questions, why didn't he contact me? Was this part of his job? To protect America's unsecured Canadian border from the "threat" of Washington-based reporters? His stumbling answers were meek at best.

The story of my misadventure in North Dakota resurfaced six weeks later when my executive producer, Joanne Levine, mentioned it in an op-ed piece about Al Jazeera for the *Washington Post.* To accompany her article, the *Post* editor retrieved an archived photo of a protest that had occurred outside Al Jazeera English's Washington studio. A group opposed to Al Jazeera coming to America—never mind that Al Jazeera Arabic already had a bureau in Washington and had been distributed in the States for years—had spent months on its website calling for a protest, claiming that the launch of Al Jazeera English could lead to suicide bombings on the streets of the United States. The group's recruitment skills were about as effective as their planning foresight. According to the *Washington Post* there were all of six protestors outside our office building, denouncing us as a "propaganda shop on American soil." A spokesman for the United American Committee—the group responsible for promoting the event—claimed that they had expected at least 200 outraged citizens to participate in what they hoped would be a continuous, round-the-clock demonstration. But by six o'clock, the band of six had gone home.[1]

I missed the show, though a few of my colleagues went by to see the protest, but like the people who had organized the demonstration, they too were disappointed with the turnout. Although a photographer covered the diminutive demonstration, the *Post* did not print a picture—until they retrieved an archived photo of the April protest to accompany Joanne's commentary. The photo's frame was tightly filled with a handful of protesters and their handmade signs, without explaining they were the protest *in toto;* from the tightly cropped photo you might have thought the demonstration was huge.

This is a strange time for America. Everywhere it seems people are seeing things through a prism of their own fears and stereotypes. When the reporter from *The Journal* in North Dakota heard that a crew from Al Jazeera English was in town, she expected Bedouins on camels. The Border Patrol assumed we were doing reconnaissance for a pending

---

1. "Al Jazeera Office Protested," *Washington Post*, May 1, 2006, p. B3.

invasion. The reporter's brother thought secret agents were marking him, but instead, the person in the mysterious car was simply designating a trail for a bike race passing through the neighborhood that weekend. The protesters believed we were bringing an anti-American agenda to the nation's capital. And my friend died in a war initiated by fears of weapons of mass destruction (WMD) and terrorist ties that didn't exist.

It doesn't take an expert to see the signs of a changing time. After being interviewed by Terry Gross on her radio program *Fresh Air* about my experiences in the war to liberate the Iraqi people, I received an e-mail from a former Israeli military officer who wrote to me: "Six months in the desert doesn't make you fucking Lawrence of Arabia." Granted.

At a time when the historic conflicts of the Middle East continue to impact us in a daily fashion—from the friends we have buried, to the news we watch every night, to the shoes we remove each time we board a plane—I am dumbfounded as to why more Americans aren't interested in the Arab world. Many Americans seem to know very little about the Middle East, and often broad-brush the whole area. When I am invited to talk, I'm often asked to describe life in Qatar, and regularly people are surprised when I tell them of the luxury hotels, fine seafood restaurants, and beautiful beaches. It seems like people in the States often picture the entire Middle Eastern region as the exploding market place often depicted in Hollywood interpretations of that part of the world.

From my vantage point—working for an Arab-based media company in the heart of the United States, trying to practice skeptical and challenging journalism in a news environment where those values seem increasingly less important—my North Dakota experience has all the elements of a good story: honest, hard-working people; fearful bureaucrats; ignorant extremists; a good soldier who made the ultimate sacrifice; and a few simple twists of fate, such as the stranger marking the brother's house and the photograph taken out of context. It was as rich and kaleidoscopic as any true picture of our country; and it was business as usual on the frontlines of America's greater jihad, and my own, personal mission Al Jazeera.

CHAPTER ONE
THE BUTTERFLY AND THE BULLDOG

I'm a Texan from a long line of Texans. When people ask how I became so interested in other people, other faiths, and other cultures, I point to my family, my education, and my experience in the Marine Corps—although perhaps not in that order.

My immediate family is one that strongly believes in civic service. Mom and Dad, Dinah and Gayland, instilled in my sister, D'Lee, and me early on the belief that we have the responsibility to repay a debt to the society we were born and raised in. My parents expected us to select a job after college from a variety of acceptable careers—military, firefighting, law enforcement, or education. We were expected to give something back and, hopefully, leave society a better place than we found it. D'Lee became a high school geography teacher in Texas, and I enlisted in the military.

My parents lead by example. Even today, Mom serves on the city council of Lone Star, Texas, and is on the governing board of her church. My sixty-three-year-old father volunteers as a firefighter in his community. When he went to firefighting school recently, he was the oldest guy there, wearing bunker gear, climbing ladders, carrying equipment up and down, the whole bit, and in the hottest month of the year.

***

Dad graduated from high school in 1961. Two weeks later, he married my mother, his sweetheart since 1951, and shipped out with the Navy the following month. Mom remained in Texas to finish her final year of high school while Dad reported to the *USS Constellation*, more familiarly known as the *Connie*. As a member of the *Connie*'s first crew, Dad sailed the world and participated in the blockade of Cuba in 1962. After a couple of years in the Navy, he switched to American Airlines, where he worked for more than thirty years, climbing his way up from a reservation agent—before the airline had computers, no less—to a mainframe computer programmer. During these three decades, he gave our family the opportunity to explore the world he had fallen in love with while at sea. But, of course, he didn't do it alone. Mom's amazing energy has always been the driving force behind our family's success and happiness. And even though she worked at the same dental office for twenty years Mom's greatest priority has always been her family.

As a child, I did my best to keep her busy. I was often rebellious and looking for trouble. When I was thirteen years old, my parents sent me to the Marine Military Academy (MMA) in Harlingen, Texas, for a few weeks during the summer in an attempt to scare some of the wild child out of me. It was as close to the real deal as a kid could get. The instructors shaved my head and treated me like I was a recruit in boot camp. My parents' goal may have been to use the threat of military service to straighten me out, but I flourished in that environment and even asked to finish high school there. Mom and Dad refused—they didn't want me to spend my final childhood years away from home—so I graduated instead from Lewisville High School in 1990.

I had been accepted to the University of Texas (UT), and Mom and Dad were ready to pay for my first semester's orientation and dorm fees. Neither of my parents had attended college and placed their hopes on my sister and me. They really wanted me to go to college; to one day wear a heavy graduation ring. But out of respect for my father, a self-made man (with Mom's help), I wanted to best him on the same field he had played on. I thought if I went to college on his dime I would spend my whole life wondering if I, too, could have made it on my own.

The desire to fulfill my civic responsibility, pay for school, and find self-transformation, together with, perhaps, some awareness that I wasn't quite ready for college, presented the military as the obvious option. My days at the MMA had left such an impression on me that I knew I was a Marine at heart, and deep inside, I felt that if I signed up with the Army, I would always wonder if I could have made it as a Marine, since the Corps has the longest, toughest boot camp. Still, I met with an Army recruiter first. The soldier I visited at the Army recruiting center had his feet on the desk and was reading the newspaper, which he would occasionally glance over to look at me as he answered my questions. The interview reinforced my preconceived notion that the Army was not as sharp and polished as the Marines, so I left and headed straight for the Marine Corps' recruiting office. I immediately told the recruiter behind the desk, Sergeant Jamal Baadani, that I wanted to be a Marine. While I've never regretted my choice of service, I have since met and worked with enough top-notch soldiers, sailors, and airmen to have a more nuanced respect for the other services.

Jamal, who is now a Gunnery Sergeant, was and continues to be what Marines call squared-away. In his mid-twenties at the time, he maintained a sharp uniform and knew how to carry himself. Instead of wooing me with benefits or career preparation for life after the service or a chance to see the world, like the other armed forces, Jamal promised me a hard time, discipline, and the profound transformation I knew I needed.

At the tender age of seventeen, I still needed my parents' permission to join the Corps, and so, as Jamal had done with so many other potential recruits, he came to our house one night to get the signatures that would seal my fate. He remembers the night as "sitting at the dinner table for two hours across from your parents—with no dinner." My mom called him a liar to his face and said the Marines would never deliver on the promises he made. She told him to get out of her house. In retrospect, I should have been the one to promise Jamal a hard time in meeting my mother and trying to convince her to let me join the Marines. My parents weren't opposed to me serving in the military, but they were dead set on me going to college right after high school.

Dad suggested Jamal and I drive around the block to give them time to privately digest our conversation. While Jamal and I were out considering our next move, Dad told Mom, who was still clinging to the dream that I would go to college and have the educational experience she missed out on, "Either we allow him to join now or he does it on his own when he's eighteen."

On October 9, 1990, the night before I was to report to Marine Corps Recruit Depot San Diego and enter boot camp, the Marines put me up in a motel in Dallas. Jamal took me to Hooters for a last hurrah and sprang for chicken wings and beer, the feast of champions. Such treatment wasn't necessarily par for the course but, as a recruiter, Jamal was grateful because my enthusiasm about joining the Corps was infectious, and a handful of my friends followed my example and enlisted as well.

Though the Marines are well known and get a lot of press, they command only about 7 percent of the military budget, and are about one-third the size of the Army. Unlike the other services, everyone who joins the Marines is first trained as an infantryman, independent of what their final assignment will be. Even if a Marine is to be a cook, he will be first trained as a rifleman, adept at dismantling and shooting an M–16 rifle. All recruits from west of the Mississippi River go to the San Diego boot camp, and that's where I stayed for three months, enduring endless physical drills and exhausting psychological pressure. In boot camp, recruits cannot use pronouns—it's one of the ways drill instructors erase their recruits' sense of individuality—and one has to ask permission before speaking: "This recruit requests permission to speak." Only at the end of training is a recruit officially called Marine and therefore allowed to refer to oneself in the first person again.

Another of boot camp's countless rules is that recruits are not allowed to take food out of the chow hall. I forgot this rule only once: I felt a cold coming on, so I pocketed a couple of oranges and kept them in my footlocker. The day I took the oranges was, coincidentally, one of the few days during training when we were allowed to call our parents. When the time came to make our calls, we all lined up. Suddenly, I was pulled out of line—the drill instructors had found my oranges—and the meanest one, always called "the heavy," spent the next couple of hours reducing me to a puddle of sweat while everyone else went to call their parents.

I guaranteed myself a rough time at boot camp by telling my superiors that I planned to be an officer and go to college. Enlisted men, as all drill instructors are, have a long history of detesting officers as pampered, blue-blood college boys who more often than not "don't know shit from Shinola." It also didn't help that I had a bulldog—the mascot of the Marines—tattooed on my left butt cheek and a tattoo of a butterfly counterbalancing the other cheek. The butterfly was weird and, not surprisingly, unwelcome, but the bulldog really got under their skins. As people who consider themselves world-class professionals at breaking others and weeding out the weak, they found it presumptuous and personally offensive that I should be so confident. They took me on as a personal challenge; an extra glint of joy shined in their eyes when I gave them cause to go after me. Nothing would have pleased these masters of pain and humiliation more than to send me packing as a civilian, with a permanent reminder of my failure forever shaming my left ass cheek.

While you're in boot camp, it's good to remember that the physical and psychological challenges just make you stronger. But it's not strength that got me through in the end. My saving grace was a dark sense of humor, born on the sweatshop floor of the quarterdeck (as a nod to their Naval heritage, Marines use nautical terms whenever possible and call the front of the large room shared by the platoon the quarterdeck; it's also where drill instructors spend one-on-one time with recruits in need of extra mentoring). Although I found it hard, salty Marines describe boot camp these days as a walk in the park in comparison to the training they endured. Boot camp used to be harsher in its physical abuse, but thanks to political correctness, now you are only pushed as hard as the weakest recruit. Boot camp builds your pride, your sense of being part of a team—even in punishment (normally we were punished all together even if only one person were at fault). Boot camp gives you a sense of invincibility, a feeling that if you can survive the drill instructors and all the challenges the training offers, then you can survive anything. To me, one of the biggest take-aways from boot camp—and of my career—wasn't as much the discipline as it was the ability to suffer and survive.

After boot camp, I was transferred to Camp Pendleton for infantry training. The physical and psychological harassment continued, but at least at this stage I was a Marine and proud to be so. That didn't stop me from putting myself in my superiors' line of fire occasionally.

Every day, the order of things seemed to be hurry up and wait. Our group of sixty brand-new Marines would rush to the .50-cal machine gun firing line, and then we'd wait an hour for our turn to fire it. Then we'd all run to the grenade tossing area, and again wait around forever for our turn to throw one. I remedied this spastic style of time management by always keeping a book in the large, mid-leg pocket of my uniform, but even that led to trouble.

One day while walking from one building to another, I was engrossed in John Steinbeck's *Of Mice and Men* and eating an apple. When I crossed paths with an officer, rather than rendering the required proper salute for an enlisted Marine—right hand straight as a board, touching the tip of your cover (Marine word for hat) with the elbow at a 45-degree angle—to all officers they see, I distractedly put the apple in my mouth pig-at-a-luau style, saluted with my left hand, and kept reading and walking. Behind me I heard an eruption of profanity. I tore away from the book just in time to have my proverbial ass handed to me by the intensely shocked and deeply offended officer, in such a way as to make Lennie, Steinbeck's childlike giant, look like Einstein compared to how I felt at the moment.

It wasn't long thereafter that I found out I wouldn't be making a career out of the infantry skills I was learning. Instead, the Marines were sending me to the Defense Information School (DINFOS) in Indianapolis. From the name of the school, I thought it would be an intelligence job, but when I arrived I was assigned to the Marines' basic journalism school. I had no idea that the military had a journalism course, and had no idea why they chose me—I excelled at math back then, not writing, which I proved throughout the course.

Journalism school was my first taste of freedom after boot camp and I did my best to take advantage of it. Our commanding officer was a crusty Marine who used to say, "When you raise young lions, sometimes you have to listen to them roar." But because of the roaring nights, I kept falling asleep during class—once, they took my chair away and I fell asleep standing up. My instructors ordered me to go to the hospital to be tested for narcolepsy. It remains the first entry in my military medical record. I suspect the only reason I graduated at all was because my instructor was teaching for the first time, and the school wasn't entirely sure if the problem was with him or me.

At my first duty station, Marine Corps Air Station Cherry Point, North Carolina, I was no better a journalist than I had been a journalism student. I kept getting in trouble for missing deadlines and turning in poorly-written stories—I was assigned such barnburners as the base gas station's grand reopening and the occasional wins of the base military police dog, Sonja, at regional police dog competitions.

Help came from who I thought at the time was the least likely of sources when Gunnery Sergeant Cliff Hill took me under his wing. Most Marines pride themselves on keeping their uniforms in immaculate condition, but Gunny Hill's uniform was anything but uniform. His shirt and trousers were from vastly different time periods, clearly discernable by their contrasting fades. He always wore camouflaged fatigues and carried a briefcase, which, when combined with his oversized, square-lens glasses held together with tape at the hinge, gave him the look of a haggard accountant walking into combat. Gunny Hill was the first of a short list of real Marine leaders who took the time to mentor me. He taught me how to write and how to get the most out of an interview.

While stationed at Cherry Point I traveled all over the world, reporting for military and civilian newspapers and acting as a liaison to the media. I then was transferred to New Orleans, where I became editor of a monthly recruiting magazine called *The Round Up*. It was a one-man editing show, with Marines at recruiting stations submitting articles. I won my first Thomas Jefferson award, a military-wide award for journalism, for a *Round Up* issue covering the bombing of the Oklahoma City federal building in 1995, where a number of military recruiters were among the 168 people killed.

In 1995, sixty-four fellow marines and I were accepted for Marine Enlisted Commissioning Education Program (MECEP). Through this program I was allowed to finally enroll at UT (five years after promising my parents, and drill instructors), where I helped train future officers while studying philosophy, religion, and ancient Greek. My areas of course study probably weren't the most career-savvy choices, but I was guaranteed a job after college: I was going to be a Marine officer.

While in college, I felt I really had an opportunity to study something meaningful, and I wanted to answer the big questions in life, which seemed to lead me back to the origins of Western philosophy and religion. Many of the core documents on those topics are in ancient Greek—all twenty-seven books of the New Testament, Plato, Aristotle, Socrates—so I studied ancient Greek. Given my situation, I had the luxury of treating university as it once was regarded, as classical education based on debate, reason, and logic, rather than as advanced job training. My transcript bears the names of many classes from UT's Religious Studies Department. For my mother, this bolstered the premonition she has held since my infancy—after I survived two bouts of Sudden Infant Death Syndrome—that I would become a priest.

In 1999, I graduated from UT with a Bachelor of Arts in classical civilization and ancient history, the first such diploma to be awarded by a newly founded hybrid program rather than a degree in divinity as my mother had hoped.

I left UT with more than just a degree in hand; I also had a ring on my finger. I met my wife, Paige, when she came out for a run with the Marines one early morning before classes to see if she was interested in the joining the Naval Reserve Officers Training Corps (NROTC) program. After dating for almost two years, she finally did join the Marine Corps, but through its spousal program rather than its active-duty ranks. When we were wed near Quantico, Virginia, my seven-year-old son, Joshua Luke (named after Paul Newman's character in the 1967 classic *Cool Hand Luke*), stood as my best man. We now have a second son, Ethan Coltrane (named after saxophonist John Coltrane, whose masterpiece, *A Love Supreme*, could be a soundtrack for our family).

After college, I attended The Basic School (TBS), on the Marine base in Quantico. TBS is every Marine officer's first (and least favorite) duty station. For six hellish months the school's instructors teach every second lieutenant the necessary leadership skills to be an infantry platoon commander and to deal with the exponential responsibilities that accompany their newly-appointed authority. In addition to weeks spent living in the woods learning combat skills, we were taught to write a "five-paragraph order," or instructions, for the troops under our command. The order outlines the details of a mission: situation, mission, execution, administration, logistics, command, and signals. Having memorized a rigid structure for passing along vital information meant that we were less likely to leave out important details when under fire, exhausted, or hungry.

The final exercise at TBS culminated in writing one such order under simulated pressure, mimicking an intense combat situation. Instructors give students the enemy's location on a map and do their best to simulate the chaos of battle: they blast heavy-metal music, project graphic images on the walls, and run through the room screaming and shooting machine gun blanks. Amidst the commotion, you have to be able to focus and write the order—the mission's success, not to mention the lives of those under your command, depend depends on it—and do it fast (students have one hour to complete the test).

This skill came in handy five years later as I sat in a soundstage in Washington, D.C., shooting my first pilot show for Al Jazeera. Although I had been interviewed many times on camera, I had never conducted interviews myself, and everything that could have gone wrong that day did. I could hear the voices of everyone in the control room in my earpiece in addition to my own delayed feedback. When the satellite feed of my co-host stopped working, we attempted to salvage the interview by cell phone. I had to steel my nerves and focus only on the task at hand—interviewing Christopher Hitchens—which I successfully did, in spite of being a new hand at it. I was told later that even seasoned hosts would have buckled under this pressure, but because of my training I didn't.

After TBS, I was slated to attend naval flight school but I failed the hearing test and did not qualify to be a pilot. Ironically, the Corps transferred me to the Miramar aviation base in San Diego anyway; not as a pilot, but as a public affairs officer.

While at Miramar, under the guidance of then-Major Steven Kay, I deployed to Kenya with the State Department. There I contributed to the African Crisis Response Initiative (ACRI), a new strategy devised by the United States on the basis of its recent experiences in Africa. In the 1990s the United States had been faced with two severe crises in sub-Saharan Africa, the bloody civil wars raging in Somalia and Rwanda. In the U.S. State Department's view, the conflicts in the two nations were similar in that they were both humanitarian crises of incredible magnitude. Although the United States approached each situation with diametrically opposed military solutions, both were met with similar results—failure. The problem of how to respond appropriately to such problems arose: if full U.S. military response (as in Somalia) and no U.S. military response (as in Rwanda) weren't the answer, then how should the United States tackle the next African crisis? ACRI became the solution. This strategy encompassed the creation of a well-trained and integrated pan-African force capable of responding to transcontinental situations.

The biggest challenge we faced in training this force was the existence of cultural and language barriers. Twenty-eight tribal languages are spoken in Kenya alone—just as an example—and we were trying to bring together soldiers from multiple African nations to act as a single pan-African military force. Along with other duties, I trained African generals to deal with the media. A brief survey of history proves, with no dearth of evidence, what can happen when a military force is not open to the media: the army's unchecked power can lead to coups d'ètat and civil wars. The military needs to stay open and be accountable to the public. One reason a military coup could not happen in the United States is because the Pentagon is under the constant scrutiny of the media. My mission, and the responsibility of any public affairs officer in fact, involved ensuring that that remained the case.

In this phase of my career I also acted as a media liaison for my boss, a Marine general and former astronaut. The job took me around the world, literally. In May 2001 some of our units deployed around the world needed a delivery of equipment, so the general decided to use the opportunity to visit his forward-stationed troops. In a four-prop plane, we took off from San Diego bound for the Eastern horizon. Twelve days later we returned from the West having circumnavigated the globe, stopping to visit troops in Spain, Kuwait,

Bahrain, Thailand, and Hawaii. The highlight of the trip for me was flying out to the *Connie*.

In a C-2A *Greyhound*, the small plane nicknamed the COD for its Carrier Onboard Delivery mission, the general, a few others, and I flew from Bahrain to where the *Connie* was floating in the Gulf. It was the only time I would get to land on a carrier, which is an experience that I'll never forget. We sat in the back of the COD, facing the rear of the plane, strapped into chairs with harnesses resembling those that NASCAR drivers wear. As the plane approached the deck of the ship, rather than slowing to land, the pilot gave it full power—this is done so that if the tail hook doesn't catch the wire stretched across the landing area, the plane will have enough power to immediately liftoff. When it does catch the cable, the resulting stop slams you into the seat as your body futilely attempts to continue its projected direction and speed of travel.

Besides the thrill of safely touching down on a swaying ship at sea, this landing was special to me for more personal reasons. The *Connie* was the ship I had heard so much about from my father. All the childhood stories he shared with me about his time on board suddenly came to vivid life, as almost nothing had changed about the carrier in the forty years since he had been there. The sailors wore the same uniforms and no one had redecorated as far as I could see. The Navy had stayed with the lots-of-iron and everything-painted-grey motif.

Our departure from the ship was no less exciting. The deck is too short for a plane to gain critical liftoff speed, so the cable used to catch the COD on the way in is now used as if it were a giant slingshot with the plane as its projectile. The two are drawn back together as far as possible and then released, shooting the plane like a rocket off the ship. Because of the COD's rear-facing passenger orientation, we were slammed against the harness with a force that feels like a sumo wrestler standing on your chest. Even with this unbelievably quick start it's still not quite enough for ascending flight, so when the plane reaches the edge of the carrier (a fraction of a second after launch) the COD drops toward the water. All of my organs that had been pinned against the front of my ribcage then shot toward my throat and my eyes strained to find the emergency exits, when the bird found its own power and lifted toward the clouds.

While at Miramar, I won my second Thomas Jefferson award for a three-part series I wrote for the base paper. The piece dealt with the difficult housing situation for the military in San Diego and was based on my own experience—I had been told that my wait for a house on base could be up to eight years, even though I was guaranteed a transfer well before that, in two to three years' time.

My next duty station was Hollywood, where I was part of the Los Angeles Motion Picture and Television Liaison Office, the Marines' liaison office with the entertainment industry. We sorted out requests to use our bases and equipment and evaluated television and film scripts to make sure they were accurate and educational—almost like producers for the U.S. government. The office has worked on such films as *Windtalkers* and *War of the Worlds*, but I worked mostly on *JAG*, a television show that I found sappy at best. They portrayed the military as always in uniform and at parade rest when not at attention; their senior officers were always shown as smarter while enlisted people were always earnestly respectful. I felt that if Norman Rockwell had written a show about the U.S. military it would have been edgier than *JAG*, and I would have liked it better. That said, the show lasted ten years, a rare feat in network television and has been aired in more than forty countries.

Some people surmise that the Marine's Los Angeles office, and each of the armed services' equivalents, is an outpost for spin or propaganda. The truth is not so black and white. Its mission is noble enough: the government recognizes the entertainment industry's influence on the public's perception and understanding of the military, and the office exists to ensure that the military in entertainment programs is depicted as accurately as possible. If a show has an educational value, then the military will provide anything from a tank to a fighter plane for its production—at cost, of course. In practice, no shortages of gray areas exist: a surprisingly small clique determines whether a movie or television show is to be supported with up to millions of dollars of equipment or personnel. Also, as most officers in the decision-making process transfer every two to three years, what these offices support or do not support can vary widely from year to year. This is particularly true for the Marines office, which has refused to follow the example of the Army, the Air Force, and the Navy, who have instituted permanent, civilian directors to their liaison offices.

One of the best examples of this is the movie *A Few Good Men*, Tom Cruise's second portrayal of a Naval officer—his first time was as a pilot in *Top Gun*, and the stylish white uniform he wears attracted lots of new recruits; ironically, most went to the Air Force, as they didn't know that the Navy also has jets. This time, Cruise plays a lieutenant assigned to defend two young Marines charged with murdering a weaker member of their squad. The lieutenant uncovers a conspiracy leading all the way to the battalion commander, played by Jack Nicholson. The film had been denied support by the office years before I worked there. I imagine the office director at the time was probably uncomfortable with a central plot about murderous Marines and a complicit commanding officer. I, on the other hand, would have supported the movie— it depicted a handful of bad apples, but it also showed the institution of the military issuing justice to even the most senior officer in charge. I was comfortable with a production showing Marines doing wrong—like it or not, it happens all the time—as long as the production also showed that justice was eventually served. While some in the Corps may be corrupt, the institution of the Corps is not. Even though I offer *A Few Good Men* as fodder for discussion, I was not involved in such contested debates. No, my fate had assigned me to oversee *JAG* as it started its slow dive into the dull abyss of its eighth and ninth seasons.

My career took a sharp turn when I again crossed paths with my recruiter, Jamal, thanks to an extraordinary event. Unbeknownst to me, *Control Room*, a documentary film featuring me had been made and shown at the 2004 Sundance Film Festival. (I discuss the film in further detail in chapter three.) At the after-party for its New York premiere a woman came up to me and said, "I'm from the Arab-American Institute (AAI) and there's someone you've got to meet. He's a Marine, he's Arab, and he's been traveling the country speaking about Arab-Americans; his name is Jamal Baadani." It had been nearly fourteen years since I had last heard that name.

I contacted Jamal again after the party. He was then living in Southern California, home to more than half a million Arab-Americans. He was not only active in the AAI but in the wake of 9/11, founded the Association of Patriotic Arab Americans in the Military (APAAM), in response to the tide of misdirected anger toward Arab-Americans caused by the attack. Jamal, who had left the Marine Corps for a brief stint as a paper millionaire in the dot-com boom only to re-enlist in the reserves just before 9/11, spoke to civic group across the country in his blue dress uniform. Referring to Arab-Americans in the military, he states: "It is our duty to reach out to our fellow citizens and fellow service members, and educate them as to who we really are." His efforts have garnered him threats from both Arabs and bigots, but also a lot of media attention, including a cover story in *Parade* magazine and a feature on CNN. Our situations were similar. He told me, "Everyone keeps telling me about this movie with you in it and I say, 'I recruited that Marine!'"

Though I had no clue when he recruited me—all I had cared about at the time was how squared-away of a Marine he was—Jamal was born in Cairo, Egypt, to Yemeni parents. When Jamal was six, his father immigrated to America to seek his fortune and left Jamal behind in the care of the Egyptian midwife who had helped deliver him. The woman had converted her one-bedroom apartment into a sort of makeshift orphanage, a place for kids she delivered whose parents could not care for them. Jamal waited for four years before his father returned for him, taking him from the midwife's crowded apartment to Dearborn, Michigan, the center of the Arab-American community in America. Eventually, Jamal's mother and siblings made it to Michigan as well. After graduating from high school Jamal joined the Corps and, as fate would have it, was deployed to Beirut, Lebanon, in 1983 when a suicide bomber blew up the Marine barracks there, killing 220 Marines. He survived the attack and went on to recruit me in 1990.

In September 2004 I visited him in Long Beach. He was proud of his accomplishments, both as a Marine and an Arab-American. He'd received a number of accolades—the Outstanding Volunteer Service Medal from the Marine Corps, the Immigrant of Inspiration Award from the National Immigration Forum—and had had his photograph taken with the likes of Senator John McCain.

Among the mementos Jamal showed me at his home in Long Beach was a video he had made during a recent trip to Cairo, a city he hadn't visited since his father brought him to the United States. The footage captures him as he walks the streets of his childhood, trying to find the apartment where he grew up. When he finally does and knocks on the door, the woman who answers is the same midwife who had raised him while his father was in the United States. Though she hadn't seen him in thirty years, she recognizes him immediately. She cries as she invites him inside the same old one-bedroom apartment. Now he sends her money and is helping to take care of her just as she took care of him.

In September 2006 the Marine Corps assigned Jamal a new mission, to serve as an expert on Arab and Muslim issues and act as a liaison between Arabs and Muslims and the Marines promoting mutual respect between Arab-Americans and Marines. As part of his job, Jamal engages the Arab media on a local level.

"That's weird, huh?" he said. "After all these years we're supposed to work together."

CHAPTER TWO
SELLING THE WAR: BEHIND THE SCENES AT CENTCOM

In spite of all the press you hear about soldiers resisting being sent to war, this rarely occurs. Marines, in particular, want to be where the action is, and I was no exception. Too many days in the make-believe world of Hollywood made me hunger for something authentic, and the Middle East was offering plenty of reality. I repeatedly requested for the Pentagon to temporarily remove me from my duties in Los Angeles and deploy me to the impending theater of war.

Finally, in the fall of 2003, Headquarters Marine Corps (HQMC) selected me for duty at the U.S. Central Command (CentCom) in Doha, Qatar.

CentCom is the command responsible for everything that the military does from Sudan to Kazakhstan, including Iraq, Afghanistan, and Iran—basically a greatest-hits list of U.S. military interests. While I was thankful for the chance to serve where the Pentagon needed me most and I regarded my assignment as an opportunity to study the culture and language of the Middle East, I felt conflicted over my high-profile assignment—I hadn't volunteered to go to Doha; I had volunteered to go to Iraq.

When I boarded the plane to Doha, I was armed with an Arabic language tape, Bernard Lewis's *What Went Wrong*, and *The Complete Idiot's Guide to Iraq, 2002 edition*—all resources I optimistically hoped would positively impact the quality of my work at CentCom. I ended up not reading Lewis's book, but I worked on my Arabic with the tape, and I devoured the idiot's guide. Maybe I shouldn't admit to reading an idiot's guide on Iraq, but I learned a lot. Actually, had someone in the administration read it, they too could have learned a lot, especially from the chapter titled: "West is West, The British and the Americans: The deal cutting, opportunism, miscalculations, and compound errors that led to a profound mistrust of the West."

In spite of the book's unfortunate title, plenty within its pages gave rise to concern about what we were planning to do in Iraq. The book recounted how many times the area had been controlled by foreign occupiers like the British, the Hashemites, the Greeks, and the Persians. I realized how likely it was that Iraqis would see what we were doing as a repeat of history: To their eyes the U.S. presence would appear as yet another attempt at colonization, as when foreign powers drew lines on a map creating a nation of people who had serious dissimilarities and no organizational reasons to be united as one nation. Clearly, as such Iraq had survived as a nation because Saddam Hussein kept everyone under lock and key.

Ironically, when I first arrived at Camp As Sayliyah, a base stuck outside of Doha and home to CentCom, I was surprised that no one spoke Arabic. Everyone who worked on my base and wasn't associated with the military was a Third Country National (TCN). They came from such places as Nepal, India, or Bangladesh seeking employment and higher wages. They were modern-day indentured servants who served our food, cleaned our toilets, and with their brooms returned the desert sand from our warehouse's cement floors to the desert landscape outside.

The base could have been a storage and distribution point for car parts as far as anyone could tell by looking at it from the outside. But on the inside, one of the warehouses was one of the world's most high-tech, communication centers from where the war would be commanded by General Tommy Franks; another warehouse contained row upon row of metal boxes, similar to the ones new cars are shipped in, which served as prison-cell–sized apartments for mid-level officers; yet another one hid large Bedouin tents—each large enough for four dozen people to bunk in—which served as sleeping quarters for lower-level personnel (including me); and inside the warehouse closest to the road was the media center from where the world would hear daily updates on the war in Iraq.

The U.S. military personnel and international journalists rubbed elbows for the next four months inside a building containing a sterile labyrinth of hastily-built offices constructed by Navy Seabees, with all the creative design elements of someone who spent their life on grey iron ships. The offices were colorless, stale, florescent-lit cubicles from hell, which was about how hot it was outside. But people in the region, where temperatures exceed 120 degrees Fahrenheit, are masters at air-conditioning. Everything was air-cooled and practically freezing, even the Bedouin tents we slept in.

My new accommodations, by war standards, were soft; Marines headed to Baghdad had no air-conditioning or shelter from the fine sand that makes its way into every crevice, but I would have given up those luxuries to be with the forward troops—a feeling any Marine left to man the bases stateside can relate to.

Although a small contingent of CentCom service members had been stationed at Camp As Sayliyah for some time, during the first couple months of 2003 the command multiplied daily as men and women selected from each of the branches of the U.S. military were deployed from different bases around the world to join CentCom's ranks in preparation for the coming engagement.

Jim Wilkinson was a notable exception; he was plucked from the ranks of Republican operatives to be appointed director of strategic communications for Franks. As such, he led the coordination of all media coverage of military actions from Morocco to Pakistan, including Operation Iraqi Freedom (OIF). Although Jim was a lieutenant in the U.S. Naval Reserves, he was given a position at CentCom that was the equivalent of a two-star general, effectively skipping five ranks and the roughly twenty-five years of service that are normally required to attain that rank.

Before Jim, Ray Shepherd, a U.S. Air Force colonel, had managed the media for CentCom. Even though Ray had been handpicked for the job after being personally interviewed by Franks and had been handling the media for the military since Jim was five years old, on orders from a *higher* command, Jim donned a uniform and became the colonel's new boss and CentCom's new communications czar. Though the fatigues Jim wore around base bore no rank, everyone knew the level of power he had. I didn't know it at the time, but this was in keeping with the larger pattern that would play out over the Iraq war: political interests trump military interests every time.

The media center the United States built in Doha beckoned journalists en masse from all over the world—Xinhua, Fox News, *The Guardian*, *Popular Science*, NPR, Al Jazeera, and many others.

When Al Jazeera's engineers showed up and started setting up equipment, I seized the opportunity to practice my wobbly Arabic. I would swing by in the morning and ask them to teach me a little of their language, and they welcomed me and my efforts. I may have been the junior officer on the media desk, but to these guys I was a military authority who was humble enough to want to learn something from them. I would often join the Al Jazeera crew for delicious lunches (they were known by all the reporters, producers, and military personnel alike for calling in the tastiest local catering) and would try out a line or two of Arabic. I also would call producers in their newsroom to test how far I could get in a conversation on the phone.

More serious conversations with Al Jazeera journalists and producers often revolved around cultural understanding. Some would say, "The Arab world has fallen behind in every measure by which you judge a society. Look at our sports, look at us in the Olympics, look at our arts, look at our literature, look at our science. It hasn't always been like this, in fact, there was a time when just the opposite was true." They wanted to hold accountable the ideologies that have caused the Arab world to lose ground; they wanted to fight against their culture's regression. This was fascinating to me; I had no idea such a struggle was going on for the Arab soul, for the very definition of what it means to be an Arab.

Some of Al Jazeera's journalists may have enjoyed my visits based on their social value, but others seemed genuinely touched that I wanted to learn about their language and culture. I was surprised to see how easy it was to shed the Ugly-American image.

I was lucky to be able to journey abroad when I was young because I had parents who recognized the educational value of overseas travel, and my dad's job with an airline certainly didn't hurt. Because of geographical and geopolitical circumstances, Americans can afford the luxury of isolationism, which often breeds the poison of provincialism. This, in turn, can lead to a fear of all things foreign. Even a small dose of international travel goes a long way toward curing this small-mindedness. It doesn't take long traveling abroad to recognize that while all humans are on many levels essentially the same and begin at similar starting points, it is the cultures we're born into, and our nearest paths to God, that lead us to different vantage points—or so it was with me.

My friend Abdullah Schleifer exemplifies this principle. He grew up in Brooklyn, wrote for the *Village Voice* in the 1950s, and, as his family name implies, was Jewish. After interviewing poet Allen Ginsberg, Schleifer decided to leave the *Voice* and travel with the Beatniks. Over the course of several years his search for fulfillment led him through revolutionary Cuba, hedonistic Paris, and finally Tunisia, to no avail. While in Tunisia Schleifer realized he was in spiritual need, and at the time, his nearest path to God was Islam. So Schleifer became a Muslim and eventually moved to Egypt. There he became the Cairo bureau chief for NBC News, and is now the Washington bureau chief for Al Arabiya. Where you're born influences your beliefs and values, but exposure to other cultures through travel and education also shapes your point of view.

As hundreds of correspondents and producers from all over the world settled in, they were assigned offices. As at any new job, or temporary headquarters, the insiders knew to jockey for the best space. The more recognizable and friendly to the United States your brand, the more room you got. The big American networks—NBC, ABC, CBS, and Fox News—got large offices to match the American viewer share each network commanded (if not the egos of the reporters and producers representing them). Everyone else got what was left.

As a result, most of the world's media sat at long communal tables in the main area, sharing laptop space. In particular, the giant Arab satellite network Al Jazeera, with up to fifty million viewers throughout the region—at the time the only nongovernmental, 24-hour news channel in Arabic—was given one of the smaller offices. The United States already had made known its displeasure over the network's coverage of the war in Afghanistan, most loudly when it bombed Al Jazeera's bureau in Kabul in 2001.

The office-space message was delivered and received loud and clear: we don't like or trust you, but as the news station of our host country we can't snub you altogether. Al Jazeera was nonplussed by this affront, and a couple of weeks later got the last laugh when it moved into a spacious corner office that had been assigned to the government of Qatar.

As the hierarchy of international reporters was established and the number of reporters in Doha increased to the point that their requests for information started to fall through the cracks, the military decided to assign personnel to each specific news agency. It became like an NFL lottery, with the more high-ranking officers saying, "I'll take Fox News," "I'll take NBC." The news networks did their part in the game by doling out swag—hats, coffee mugs, and T-shirts—in an effort to recruit the spokesperson of their choice—the person they believed might give them the best access. I got ABC, the European Broadcasting Union, and China's Xinhua News. Frank Thorp, the Navy captain who was my mentor and direct superior in Doha, recognized my interest in Al Jazeera, "You've got a pretty good relationship with the Arab guys, why don't you take the Arab press?"

I took this as a sign of appreciation and faith in my capacities: this was an important assignment for a junior spokesperson and a junior officer. Looking back on it, it also revealed how much strategic forethought the military had put into how we were going to address our action in the Arab world. Zero. CentCom assigned the junior guy to be America's face on the Arabic network that had a near monopoly on the Arab world's attention. In my view, things should have been planned very differently. Long before Thorp and I were in Doha, back when the Pentagon and CentCom Headquarters in Florida were still planning this operation and their strategists were asking themselves how many boots would be needed on the ground and which places would be bombed during "Shock and Awe," someone should have asked, "Who's taking Al Jazeera? Who's going to speak to the Arab world for us?"

Me.

Over time, as I developed a working relationship with Al Jazeera, I realized that the station was a real news organization and not a front company for anti-American propaganda, as the U.S. administration would have us believe. Like the other journalists working from the media center, Al Jazeera's correspondents were trying to do their job and get the story, but unlike some of the journalists in Doha, the story seemed to be more important to them for its inherent social purpose rather than their own career ambitions.

Al Jazeera's reporters ran the gamut socially and politically, a fact that was lost on many of my coworkers at CentCom. Al Jazeera was composed of Islamists and Ba'athists, but also in its ranks were progressives, and just good, old-fashioned cynics as well. A shared professional mission and, more importantly, a sense of Pan-Arabism united them. Slowly I began to see and understand the meaning and depth of it all. Although their reporters differed enough on the surface—the diversity and distinctiveness of their journalistic voices rivaled those in any Western station—underneath they were Arabs covering a war against other Arabs. I still thought in my typical American way that a Palestinian wouldn't feel an Iraqi's suffering, but the truth would soon be brought painfully home to me.

One of their journalists, Omar Al Issawi, made a striking impression on me. He was very well informed and culturally open to criticism. He could point out candidly where the Arab world was failing as well as where the United States was failing. Omar had a modern, trendy air to him, a biting intellect, and a deep knowledge of cultures—both his and mine. He could have been a young hip intellectual in New York City.

Omar is Lebanese, very well educated, and speaks perfect English. He had been a star reporter for Al Jazeera in Afghanistan before leaving the network to direct his own documentary films. Omar was lured back into reporting for Al Jazeera because the network gave him a great opportunity as the Al Jazeera point man at CentCom. He was the guy I talked to every day, and he attempted to explain the Arab world to me.

Omar also expressed curiosity about the U.S. point of view, and it occurred to me that if he wanted to explain the American side of the story to the Arab population, I should try to give him access. My recommended approach was one of strategic limited engagement: find the most progressive person and give him all the access he needs.

I thought that Omar should have been next to Franks when he was planning things such as relief or civil affairs efforts, and that Omar should have traveled with Franks when he visited the troops on the ground. Behind closed doors I argued to my superiors that Omar had credibility in the eyes of the Arab world that I would never know as a military spokesperson. I urged my chain of command to take advantage of Omar's platform to get their message to the Arab street.

I asked Franks to call on Omar first at a press conference as a sign of respect to the Arab world, to which the general replied, "Sure, right after I rip off his head and shit down his throat!" I took that as a no.

To Fox News viewers, which described the majority of my CentCom colleagues, Al Jazeera was a hostile network, and its portrayal of the United States's actions frustrated my superiors, who would be outraged at the station's reporting and vow to cut off all access to its reporters.

I would argue that time on Al Jazeera's airways—for better or worse—gave CentCom our only opportunity to reach the audience we most needed to reach: the Arab people. My ideas on the subject were clear: look beyond the battle for Iraq; we were dealing with the larger war on terror, and if we didn't reach a broader audience, we were going to lose the war. We may have preferred the easy, pre-digested interviews, but I felt that the more challenging interviews that Al Jazeera served us most significantly impacted our national security: Al Jazeera offered us a chance to engage the ideologies that fueled 9/11.

As important as getting news back home might be, the folks from Minnesota or Nevada didn't board planes with box cutters. I argued my case so strongly that at one point an Air Force lieutenant colonel came to me and said, "Check your uniform and see what name is on it. You need to remember which side you're on." It wouldn't be the last time I would be accused of being a traitor.

But no amount of insistence that we needed a more robust international focus could shift Jim's focus from the American media. He was a master tactician at shaping perception and ran the entire media operation like a political campaign—and non-Americans didn't get a vote. His methods call to mind the cliché that truth is the first casualty of war, but, honestly, at CentCom that would have been an overstatement. That would imply that we thought about the truth. It's not that I was asked or ordered to lie—I wasn't—but we weren't having many discussions about the nature of truth either, and to do so would have been as out of place as bringing up an Abrams tank in a philosophy class.

It was easy to see that Secretary of Defense Donald Rumsfeld considered the media an adversary—and one that would best be contained—from the way he dealt condescendingly with the press corps. Even at one of the very first press conferences after the invasion in Iraq, he responded to a reporter by correcting his grammar instead of answering his question.

By April 11 he had turned to criticizing those who would criticize the war effort. "I picked up a newspaper today and I couldn't believe it," he chastised reporters at a Pentagon news conference that day. "I read eight headlines that talked about chaos, violence, unrest. And it was just Henny Penny—'the sky is falling.' I've never seen anything like it! And here is a country that is being liberated, here are people who are going from being repressed and held under the thumb of a vicious dictator, and they're free."

Given this attitude, we at CentCom were out to control information, shape it, and overload the airwaves with it. "Every minute we're on the air, the enemy isn't." Jim delivered this message to his military public affairs officers continuously at CentCom—after all, he had seen this tactic successfully employed in Florida against the Democrats during the 2000 presidential election. If we were on air, the war's critics, to say nothing of the enemy, weren't. To the U.S. military, the enduring lesson of Vietnam—where the U.S. military lost a war without ever having lost a battle—is that only the will of the American people can defeat the U.S. military. Jim had learned from his years as a Republican operative that the will of the American people was up for grabs.

To implement this approach, first Jim envisioned a backdrop: with the help of a set designer from New York, CentCom constructed a $200,000 stage just for U.S. generals to give briefings from. Then, the spokespeople were all given a daily schedule of calls to make to radio stations around the United States. Once a week, some station in Topeka would receive a phone call from their favorite captain in Doha, who would check in with the wacky morning radio show to let them know how the war was going, even though that captain was hundreds of miles from the war itself.

Another task was to feed the messages of the day to the reporters at the media center, to let the world know why the United States was about to go to war. These talking points flowed directly from the White House Office of Global Communications to the military press officers in Doha, who then repeated them incessantly to the press.

The administration was taking no chances: everyone, from the lieutenants on the frontlines on up to the President of the United States, had to be on the same page. Again, this kind of disciplined messaging had won President George W. Bush the election. Maybe now it would win him a war.

This dogmatic devotion to the message was new to me, but for Jim it was business as usual. Whereas the Corps encouraged its young officers to challenge assumptions as a requirement for success or at least survival, it seemed the Republican Party must have rewarded unquestioning commitment. It's an understatement to say Jim drank the Kool-Aid; when it came to the Bush–Cheney party line, Jim was intravenously mainlining the Kool-Aid.

Jim and I were roughly the same age and, like me, he had grown up in a small Texas town. We were both compelled to serve our nation, but where I took the military route, Jim took the partisan one. He had worked his way up from spokesperson in the office of Republican Congressman (and President Bill Clinton nemesis) Dick Armey to a full-on operative for the 2000 Bush campaign. Jim was the one who burnished and then disseminated the notion that Al Gore had claimed to have invented the Internet. He played a major role in the fracas of the Florida recount for the 2000 election, practicing the kind of guerrilla politics Karl Rove admires. Jim was the spokesperson for what would become known as the "Brooks Brothers Riots," in which a group of nattily attired, young, congressional staffers stormed the offices of the Dade County canvassing board, thus stymieing the recount efforts. Jim later described the affair to the press as a spontaneous and emotional event, rather than as an organized incident that might legally constitute criminal intimidation.

Once Bush took office, Jim was named Deputy Director of Communications for Planning in the White House. He helped coordinate the president's visit to Ground Zero on September 14, 2001, and Jim handed Bush the bullhorn through which he shouted to the men digging through the rubble, "I can hear you. The rest of the world hears you. And the people who knocked down these buildings will hear all of us soon." That moment became a symbol and a huge boost for the Bush administration, and Jim had helped orchestrate it.

Then in the summer of 2002 Jim became a charter member of the White House Iraq Group (WHIG), a pick-up team of Republican operatives brought together to devise the sell of the Iraq war to the American public. Bush's chief of staff Andrew Card organized the small but influential team that included Karl Rove, Karen Hughes, Mary Matalin, Nicholas Calio, Condoleezza Rice, Stephen Hadley, I. Lewis "Scooter" Libby, and Jim. It seems some believed that selling the war also included undermining its critics. All of the above listed members of the WHIG, with the possible exception of Nicholas Calio, were subpoenaed in the investigation into who leaked to the press Valerie Plame's once covert status as a Central Intelligence Agency (CIA) spy. Plame's husband, Joseph Wilson, was a former U.S. ambassador and critic of the administration's WMD intelligence.

According to a senior White House official quoted in a front page story in the *Washington Post*, the group met on a weekly basis in the Situation Room, planning speeches and white papers—all while denying its very existence or purpose.[1] As White House Chief of Staff Andrew Card famously told a reporter from the *New York Times* the summer before the invasion, "From a marketing point of view, you don't introduce new products in August."

Straight from the message laboratory of the WHIG, Jim moved into place to implement the plan at CentCom, where he found a willing group of press hungry for information. Many of the reporters seemingly had traded in their journalistic skepticism for full-on, support-the-troops cooperation, even if "the troops" meant someone like me, armed with my handy White House-blessed talking points. Perhaps any desire U.S. reporters had to challenge the way things were run at CentCom paled when confronted with the opportunity for a career-defining, scud-stud moment in the sun. They knew a

---

1. Barton Gellman and Walter Pincus, "Depiction of Threat Outgrew Supporting Evidence," *Washington Post*, August 10, 2003, pg. A1.

reporter's career could take a star turn during war. This was as much their war as it was any Marine's.

I was the youngest officer on the press desk and the low man on the totem pole, but I was one of a few picked to give television interviews. After receiving the speaking points for the day, I would head out for a round of interviews. Before going on air, the reporter often would ask if I had any messages I wanted to get out. Sure, I would rattle off the buzz words—regime change, WMD, ties to terrorism—and the journalist would script his interview around a lieutenant's reasons for going to war.

When a reporter asked before the invasion, "Why are you going to invade Iraq?" the only honest answer I could have given was, "The U.S. military will invade Iraq if, and only if, the President orders us to."

When you are in uniform, you don't pick and choose your battles; you do as directed. There are no other justifications. It's not the military's place to explain or defend an order— that's a politician's job. In military circles, commenting on something beyond your purview is called getting outside your lane. It's something you hear a lot in military media training: stay in your lane.

The public affairs training at Fort Meade also taught us that we weren't supposed to spin things. There's a difference between public affairs and public relations (PR). Military public affairs officers are meant to inform the general public, through the media, of military action, but not to explain the reasoning behind it. A public affairs officer's mission was clear: "Maximum disclosure, minimum delay." Public affairs officers are not designed to do PR; and they certainly aren't supposed to do propaganda. That job was reserved for politicians and their flacks—people in suits, not uniforms.

At CentCom we were sliding across the line from public affairs into PR by talking more about ideology, message, and context rather than the facts. Who believes a political flack? When a politician says something to the press the viewer knows they have an agenda, but the military is supposed to be nonpartisan, putting out information the viewer knows is straight.

I argued with Jim—and, unlike a two-star general, and to Jim's credit—he let me. "We should release the facts, the events exactly as they happened, or as close to it as we can afford to reveal. Not messaging. Did I miss the class on *messaging* at DINFOS?" Jim argued we needed to provide context so people could understand a story's significance, because if we didn't, someone else would. The word *context* was like a mantra for him. "We're not providing spin," he would insist. "We're providing context. Facts without context are meaningless."

The press may not have realized it at the time (and in retrospect I sometimes wonder just what they did realize) but this was a precedent: the arguments may have been tired, but to have a lieutenant argue on national and international television why America needed to invade a sovereign nation was new. The military isn't a partisan organization; it doesn't decide why our nation goes to war, only how. And while the Pentagon may have played along with propaganda efforts in previous wars—General Westmoreland constantly referred to the popular support U.S. troops enjoyed in Vietnam—frontline soldiers generally were noncommittal, at best, as to the rationale for fighting, and ill-informed, at worst.

But there I was, a young lieutenant from Texas saying, "Saddam Hussein is a Hitler" and "Saddam has violated international law for long enough." At the end of the interview, the reporter would pat me on the back and thank me for my service. ("Back to you, John.") Then, I would move on to the next camera station and repeat exactly the same thing, over and over again, day after day.

I didn't realize at the time that the messages I believed to be true were often more tried than true. They were a paradigm the government had used over and over to sell war. In his book *War Made Easy*,[2] Norman Solomon lists the lines the U.S. government has used on the media in every war since Vietnam: "This guy is a modern day Hitler"; "This is about human rights"; "They are the aggressors, not us." As I scanned the list I could hardly believe how many of the phrases I had used.

While I do not regret the military information we were (or weren't) giving reporters at CentCom, my feelings about the larger talking points—the messages of the day—that I was given to dispense are more complex.

Take WMD, for example. I spent a lot of my own time reading about the myriad inspection teams that went into

_____

2. Norman Solomon, *War Made Easy* (John Wiley & Sons, 2006).

Iraq: United Nations (UN) Special Commission (1991–1999), UN Monitoring, Verification and Inspection Commission (1993–2002), and the International Atomic Energy Agency—all different organizations with different acronyms that kept going back in different years, all apparently failing to prove or disprove the existence of WMD for different reasons. I could list all of them and say with confidence that they had worked with due diligence. But why, if no WMD existed in Iraq, had these teams been consistently thwarted in their efforts? Saddam continually played cat-and-mouse games with the inspectors. Why would he go to the trouble and risk a military invasion if he wasn't hiding something?

I also spent a lot of time parrying over the terms "occupation" and "empire." I would say, "We are not going to be an occupying force, we want to turn this thing over to the Iraqis as soon as possible." Or, "This is not an extension of an empire." And a reporter, usually foreign, would respond, "Well, you have military troops in 60 countries around the world." But that's not an empire. An empire, as defined by the *American Heritage Dictionary of English Language*, is a political unit having an extensive territory or comprising a number of territories or nations and ruled by a single supreme authority.[3] At the time of the Iraq invasion, the

---

3. Definition of empire: *The American Heritage® Dictionary of the English Language, Fourth Edition.* Houghton Mifflin Company, 2004, accessed January 4, 2007. Dictionary.com http://dictionary.reference.com/browse/empire.

United States had more troops in Germany than in any other country except the United States, and Germany officially opposed the invasion of Iraq, a far cry from "being ruled by a single supreme authority." But the answer to the question of whether the United States was an occupying force, is easy: it was and continues to be. I was wrong to argue otherwise.

Before the first bullet was ever fired, our office had already engaged in the information war on every front. In the evenings I was charged with logging into chat rooms where people were talking about the war—websites run by the *International Herald Tribune*, MTV, even Oprah.com. Here I honed the broader arguments surrounding the war. I soon recognized that only a limited number of arguments persisted against the war. Even if they were worded in a variety of ways and came from different places, in terms of logic they all fell along a handful of common lines.

I researched those arguments and found enough information to support any side of any argument—including my own. I'd find postings like:

> After America's best troops have put their life on the line to "free" Shi'ite Muslim fundamentalists, the U.S. military will have to stay 20 years or more to keep terrorists from taking over the country that we opened up to them. Isn't there better things that Americans could be doing for the world? (signed Dave25).

To which I'd respond:

"Dave, thanks for engaging. This is important stuff. As to your comment: 1. It would not just free up Shi'ites. It would liberate all Iraqi people—Shi'ite, Sunni, Kurds, Christians, etc. 2. America's best troops already put their lives on the line every day in Iraq. It's called Operation Southern Watch, protecting the Shi'ites from the wrath of Saddam's military below the 33rd parallel, and Operation Provide Comfort, protecting the Kurds above the 36th parallel." (Signed CentComsprsn).

Only later did I realize that my e-mails must have come across like Big Brother, especially when I mentioned their name in my reply. However unintentionally, I was telling them: I read your message, I'm with the government, I see what you're saying in this chat room, and you're not so anonymous after all.

Everyone has bigger balls on the Internet, but I think when an actual government spokesperson uses your name and zeroes in on you, even the least paranoid chat room participant might wonder, "Just how much do they know about me?"

How much did I believe the arguments I was making? For the most part, I really did. I believed the United States was (and is) not an empire. I believed enough what-ifs existed to justify going into Iraq. Saddam could have possessed WMD; enough evidence existed between his prior possession of them and his antics with the inspection teams to justify reasonable doubt. He could have had ties to terrorists, especially if you buy into what seems to pass as the current definition of a terrorist as any nonstate player with harmful intentions toward the United States. I also believe Saddam was a plague on his people. And when Secretary Colin Powell spoke before the UN and laid out what were supposed to be the facts, I printed out his speech to make sure our whole office was on the same sheet of music. Maybe I was the one who drank the Kool-Aid.

My biggest concern about the administration's justification for invasion was that the government went all in on WMD. And when the weapons couldn't be found, the message shifted, further undermining our credibility.

Our military strategy also concerned me. I knew military strategists planned for a race to Baghdad. Not that it was my place to do so, but I was curious, so I asked a senior military officer involved in implementing the invasion: "As we rush through the country knocking out the Ba'athist headquarters in each town along the way, what are we leaving in their place? How do we so rapidly set up local governments as we go?"

I remember the guy I asked, and I remember his smile. "Nothing," he said. "We're not worried about that."

Maybe he believed that the Iraqis were going to organize themselves. But I was worried about the vacuum we were leaving in our wake. I had optimistically assumed that we had a good plan for Baghdad—until I went to Baghdad and saw what was happening.

From the stale warehouse of the media center I watched U.S. forces hundreds of miles away storm into Iraq and felt a naïve envy and youthful frustration at being left behind.

Regret for not being closer to the story was a bond I shared with most reporters at CentCom, who spent their long, long days with us—although they retired each evening to five-star international hotels on Qatar's coast. Even before the initial invasion, most of the A-Team (including NBC's Tom Brokaw and ABC's George Stephanopoulos) had moved on; it didn't take them long to realize CentCom wasn't going to provide any real information. Many of those who remained were the up-and-comers, reporters looking for a special moment that would progress their careers. But we sewed things up so tight there wasn't much room for error on our part or improvisation on theirs, and the reporters' dreams of Dan Rather glory—challenging the man behind the podium, cracking the façade of transparency we had created—seemed more and more remote with the passage of each identical day. Desperation was in the air. There was an edgy sense coming from the press of, "I *need* information!"

Everyone had expected a first-day press conference on March 23, 2003, announcing the start of ground operations; they wanted Franks to do what General Norman Schwarzkopf had done in Gulf Storm. But that didn't happen; there was just silence. No press release from us. No talking points. One hour went by, two hours went by—and the reporters, like children on Christmas morning with no presents, were beside themselves. Forty-eight hours passed, and still nothing. CentCom was in complete radio silence. The press knew we had crossed the line of attack; their embedded reporters told them as much, and they even had pictures to prove it. For our part, we didn't want to walk down the hall for fear of getting caught in an L-shaped ambush of furious reporters.

What the reporters didn't know was that we were as frustrated as they were. We didn't volunteer to leave our families and homes to sit in the desert, 500 miles away from the war and not do our jobs. We wanted to be great public affairs officers almost as badly as they wanted to be Edward R. Murrow circa 1940 in London. Tensions were definitely high.

Slowly, we started giving out information, but only sparingly and on Jim's (read: administration's) terms. The mood had changed from the kind of anger you might get from prisoners you were starving to that of prisoners you were feeding crumbs, and stale ones at that. For example, during his daily press conference on April 10, 2003, Brigadier General Vincent Brooks displayed the now-famous pack of playing cards issued to American ground troops featuring the faces of Saddam and fifty-one of the Coalition's most wanted. This revelation was equally surprising to us public affairs officers, as it was our first time hearing of the cards as well. Thorp's instincts in these situations were always dead-on. Like they say animals do before an earthquake, the hair on Thorp's ears raised. Sensing a tsunami of anxiety about to explode from the hundred-plus reporters at this briefing, he wrote on his small pad for an officer standing beside him to see, "We're screwed."

With military skills that would have served General Custer well, Thorp, eyeing the back door, began devising a plan for a hasty exit strategy. When Brooks stepped down from the podium with the deck—the *only* deck—in his pocket and disappeared off the media center's radar, Thorp was ready. In a moment as close as a media liaison will ever get to deserving a bronze star for life-saving action, Thorp led a charge of public affairs officers for the door into our private back office. No man was left behind.

The ensuing frenzy spoke volumes about how little these reporters were getting that was actually worth reporting. The cards were not a novel concept. In fact, decks have long been printed and used as learning tools to help service members commit information to memory—but for every reporter that day—a day in which people were dying and U.S. troops were closing in on an ancient Arab capital—the deck of playing cards they had not seen up close was the lead story.

Michael Wolff, then media columnist for *New York* magazine, arrived at Doha in this environment. Wolff may not have known much about covering a war but he knew a good media story when he saw one, and he was watching one on his television in New York every day. He had listened to the spin we were selling, looked at the high-tech stage from which uniformed men found new ways to literally say nothing, and convinced his editors that he needed to be there, just to write about what wasn't happening. ("It is not just that the general and his staff and the military communications people seem secretive or averse to supplying information," he wrote, "it's that they don't seem to know what information is. The press office wouldn't even provide the *Newsweek* correspondent with the first name of one of the generals."[4]) And after hearing tales of the reporters' high-school behavior—the competition for office space among the bigwigs, the no-name reporters forced to share the cheap seats on the long rows of tables in the Bill Mauldin Mezzanine, and the daily scramble for good seats in the briefing room, the better to get called on by teacher—he took his shot.

"I mean no disrespect," he asked Brooks one morning, live on international television, "but what is the value proposition? Why are we here? Why should we stay? What's the value of what we're learning at this million-dollar press center?"[5] His comment might not have been so galling to those in charge of handling the media if all the other reporters hadn't hooted and hollered along. And Wolff clearly enjoyed his moment with a smirk on his face that said, *Gotcha.* He had come all this way to ask this one smartass question, and the unflappable Brooks reminded Wolff that information was coming out of a lot of places, such as the Pentagon and Iraq, and he was, as all the reporters were, free to go at any time.

---

4. "Live from Doha," *New York Magazine*, April 7–14, 2003.
5. "My Big Fat Question," *New York Magazine*, April 21, 2003.

Wolff's wisecrack made him persona non grata at Cent-Com, though he was much of the rank-and-file's hero. He fielded congratulations from numerous reporters for days afterwards—and received 3,000 hate e-mail messages from Rush Limbaugh's listeners. (Limbaugh had played Wolff's comments on his radio show, given out the columnist's e-mail address, and basically said, "Sic 'em.").

But Jim ripped Wolff the hardest. Jim pulled Wolff out of the building and said, according to Wolff's column, "I have a brother who is in a Hummer at the front, so don't talk to me about too much fucking air-conditioning. . . . A lot of people don't like you. Don't fuck with things you don't understand. This is fucking war, asshole. No more questions for you."

"I had been warned," Wolff wrote in his column, and recalled his encounter with Jim to other members of the press. "'You've met the Hitler Youth,' said another reporter. Everybody laughed. This was grim but it was funny. The camaraderie of people who understood the joke—who were part of the joke—was very reassuring and comfortable."

I wasn't there when Jim lit into Wolff, but Jim talked about it afterward. As I remember the story, he also threatened to punch Wolff in the mouth, but this could have been the legend growing, because Wolff failed to mention it in his column—surely a fact too juicy for a guy like Wolff to pass up. Then Wolff went back and wrote his column, describing Jim as "an Uber-civilian . . . although he was a civilian he was inexplicably in uniform—making him, I suppose, a sort of paramilitary figure."[6] Jim loved the story; he showed it with delight, the kind with which others share pictures of their children. Jim prided himself on playing hardball with the press. The Bush administration has a real disdain for the media, and it seemed Jim's sentiments came straight from the top.

We were handing out a lot of information, but it was contextual information that contributed to a larger picture of war operations. Wolff chose not to see it in that context. He wanted to come in and act like this was the entire world of military–media relations. The media center was a target-rich environment for a guy like that.

At CentCom we were responding in an ever-evolving situation to a new type of war reporting from embedded reporters, and asking ourselves, "What's the right thing to do here? How much can we say without putting someone at risk?" Wolff never gave anyone credit for asking that question. Wolff, for instance, was bothered that we were always telling reporters, "We won't discuss military operations."

This is a key issue. The U.S. military never discusses imminent or ongoing military operations for the simple reason that they don't want to give information to the wrong listeners and endanger troops' lives. If Marines were going to move through say, Fallujah, we wouldn't talk about their operation until they were through the city, the mission was ended, and everyone was safe, even if an embedded reporter

---

6. "My Big Fat Question."

had been caught in the middle of a firefight. Obviously, embedded reporters were prohibited from releasing sensitive information such as present location, details regarding future actions, or anything else that could put the troops at risk. But they didn't always abide.

CentCom was unwavering on this point because we knew Saddam's people were listening to all our transmissions and were watching Western channels to get their news. Western reporters who had been in and out of Baghdad for years told me the Iraqi minister of information Muhammed Saeed Al Shahaf would always mention stories that they had filed after they left Baghdad. We had to be careful about what information we gave out because we knew our enemy was paying close attention.

During the first Iraq war, Operation Desert Storm, the military distributed information at the CentCom level from General Schwarzkopf's podium. Rather than embedded reporting, which hadn't been conceived yet, the U.S. military used pool reporting to share information with journalists. One reporter would be escorted out on the ground and shown something great—and then told to share it with his or her fellow reporters. The media, of course, hated the system. General Schwarzkopf gave daily briefings that would explain the smart-bomb attacks and bloodless battles—his public affairs officers enjoyed great success controlling the release of information. As Michael Deaver, President Ronald Reagan's former media strategist, said at the time, "If you were going to hire a public relations firm to do media relations for an international event, it couldn't be done any better than it is being done."

In OIF Franks didn't like the press and wanted as little to do with them as possible. But more important, he was concerned about the sensitive, tactical information already coming out from the embedded reporters. If CentCom gave out a strategic picture, it could serve as a blueprint for connecting all the dots the embedded reporters were releasing. This was never an issue in the pool reporting because when General Schwarzkopf gave out "new" information, it concerned operations that were already over. At CentCom in 2003, we didn't have that luxury.

As nearly all forward units had reporters with them, news organizations had access to news instantaneously, in real time. They even knew about military operations long before we did, because the information took a while to work its way up to CentCom. The informational chain of command goes from the squad to the company to the battalion to the regiment to the division to the service to the land forces command, and finally to CentCom. An embedded reporter from NBC, for example, would show a Bradley fighting vehicle on fire—when all the other stations would see it on television they would want to cover it also, but without crediting NBC, so they would call us to confirm it. At first we tried to chase down the information by trying to contact forward units, but after a while we would say, "Just attribute each other, would you? Tell your viewers you saw it on NBC."

Calls for confirmation may have annoyed us in the Media Center but the potential broadcast of sensitive information by an embedded reporter in the field made us lose sleep at night. Although I'm sure other networks weren't blameless, Fox News, ironically, earned the worst reputation for their carelessness with Department of Defense (DoD) ground rules for embedded media—and possibly Coalition lives. At one point during the early days of the invasion, Fox News aired a clip of one of their reporters, embedded with the Army, beside an Abrams tank that had been hit, discussing the sequence of events in detail. Abrams tanks are supposed to be indestructible in this type of warfare but at the time the tank apparently had a weak spot in the tracks. A rocket-propelled grenade (RPG) had hit the right spot and started a fire that disabled the tank. The reporter was showing the fire, and explaining, live, where the weak spot was. A lot of military people watching said, "He just gave instructions on how to take down one of our most valuable vehicles and put the guys inside at risk." So if you were a Fedayeen soldier and didn't know that much about the Abrams tank you might say, "Oh, I should save my RPG shot until I can get around to the side. Thanks, Fox News!" (This Achilles Heel has since been remedied.)

On another occasion, during a live broadcast on Fox News, Geraldo Rivera, who was embedded with the 101st Airborne Division, drew a map in the sand for his viewers, showing where they were in Iraq and where they were headed. It was the kind of report that young Iraqi intelligence officers would have been promoted for. According to the rules of embedding, he should have been removed from the country. He was indeed ordered to leave Iraq because of the report, but the power of celebrity, even the goofy kind of celebrity Geraldo enjoys, has a way of overcoming such pedestrian rules and he was allowed to remain at the request of the 101st Airborne's commanding general.

The amount of tactical information that can be released to journalists before the enemy can piece together a jigsaw puzzle that reveals an all-too-telling intelligence picture challenges military leaders at a strategic level—and no strategic command had ever dealt with the embed quandary before. The answer in these situations is always to err on the side of caution. Hence, we weren't going to say one thing that would put a troop's life at risk.

I am now less conflicted by the information we at the CentCom media center didn't put out than I am about some of the information that we did.

Marines teach you to do the right thing for the right reason. I didn't lie or give misinformation, and I was not asked to lie. I like to believe that if I had I been asked to give information I knew was false, I would have refused and faced prosecution. But between truth and falsehood lies a vast grey area, and considering the spin CentCom was releasing, we were deep in that gray area.

CHAPTER THREE
BRINGING WAR INTO YOUR LIVING ROOM

Long before the Bush administration decided to use men and women in uniform to deliver their message, the U.S. networks were on board—their love affair with the military was strong as ever. "I think Navy SEALs rock," Katie Couric told a Navy commander at the end of a wartime interview on the *Today Show* in April 2003. Smart bombs were smarter than ever and war was a clean affair.

After all, nothing captivates an audience more than war, which boosts ratings and generates an endless supply of breaking news stories. CNN's viewership spikes during wartime, and interestingly, those viewership levels don't come down after the spike as far as they were before the war; they plateau a little higher than before. But to sustain the momentum, viewers' hunger must be fed. That's why Fox News touts "breaking news" even when there isn't any, or why Wolf Blitzer mans CNN's *Situation Room* even when there is no situation.

The business of television news is just that, of course. Someone from CNN may say in public, "I don't care what kind of ratings Fox is getting with its pro-American angle." But in the boardroom—where they feel the combined effect of the very real need to produce for the shareholders, whether those shares be of Time-Warner, NewsCorp, Disney, or GE, and of the Bush administration's very effective campaign to equate any skepticism about the war in Iraq with a lack of patriotism—they're saying something else. The combination of these two elements form the makings of a massive failure of will on the part of the media.

During the invasion of Iraq, MSNBC packaged its news with the slogan "Our Hearts Are With You." They were referring to the troops, I guess, but at that point the audience at home could have used the reporters' brains instead.

The media's role in the United States's disconnect between the romanticism and the realities of war was evidenced during the first Gulf war, or Operation Desert Storm. To Americans, Operation Desert Storm is Whitney Houston singing the National Anthem, jets flying in formation over sporting events, returning soldiers being showered with praise and confetti (a hero's homecoming for a hundred-hour war), and Lee Greenwood's song, "Proud To Be An American." Video clips of the smart bombs that seemed to travel down elevator shafts and practically knock on the doors of their intended victims—bad guys all—before blowing them to smithereens were replayed over and over. General Schwarzkopf, America's beloved "Stormin' Norman," ran his press briefings like a pro, but the public even fell in love with Colin Powell, a man of quiet conscience, as he tried to stay out of the limelight.

Most Americans, however, have no memory of the battle scenes and war dead because the U.S. media had already begun its sanitization of war. Although U.S. casualties were light (fewer than 500; 147 of those were battle-related deaths), untold thousands of Iraqis (estimates of 100,000 killed and 300,000 wounded are not uncommon) lost their lives as they fled Kuwait. Images of the carnage have gone largely unseen in the U.S. media even though some of the burned-out trucks and tanks that Coalition forces bombed on what came to be known as the Highway of Death in Kuwait are still there. (For months after the war ended, charred remains of Iraqi soldiers could be seen still inside those vehicles.)

As a result, thirteen years later, when the United States said it was time to go to war with Iraq again, many Americans began to hum the Lee Greenwood song as they prepared to send their loved ones to war.

By withholding the images that chronicle the true human cost of war—whether those dead and injured be soldiers, the "collateral damage" of civilian casualties, or enemy combatants like the incinerated driver stuck in the sand beside the Highway of Death, cigarette still between his blackened lips—the media runs the risk of infantilizing its audience and sugarcoating a harsh truth. Other than the men and women in uniform the United States bid farewell to in 2003, life resumed as normal for most Americans, with no day-to-day sacrifices to be made—no one was being told to recycle metal for weapons, to buy war bonds, or certainly to enlist and go to war. And why should they, after the mission was declared accomplished by the president, dressed in a flight suit on an aircraft carrier so close to the coast of California that cameramen had to be careful not to get San Diego's beautiful skyline in the shot—all less than six weeks after the war began?

The Pentagon barred photographs of flag-draped coffins returning from Iraq, but the media censored itself when it came to showing images of war-wounded civilians and soldiers alike. Reporters in Iraq told me that their networks regularly refused to run the grisly images they sent in, saying their audiences didn't want to see them. (Similar decisions were made in the United States after 9/11, as Americans in some markets were deprived of images of people leaping to their deaths from the World Trade Center towers, footage that was quite common overseas.)

In America we like to say we cherish freedom of the press. We justly claim it as one of the blessings of democracy and look down on societies where the governments control the media, but in reality the United States has lost ground on these freedoms. And U.S. networks have resorted to tiptoeing around some issues for fear that American audiences will not stomach tough questions about foreign policy or the administration during a time of war, even the possibly endless war on terror.

The business model of the U.S. networks allows—encourages even—the audience to shape the medium. Fox News started the trend, capitalizing on the conservative audience that built talk radio, but CNN and the other news networks have followed on their coattails. The television network and the audience together have become a political force. In Iraq, the government counted on the networks not saying anything too critical or questioning, particularly about the troops. The media offices of the Bush administration exploited that patriotism, and presented their arguments for the war in an environment where they wouldn't have to sustain a lot of critical questions. Government officials preyed upon the American people's guilt, a lingering casualty of the Vietnam War, harbored from the treatment of returning U.S. veterans. Stuck between a rock and a hard place, the reporters seemingly decided not to question service members, young troops like me, who were giving the reasons for the invasion—a calculated error.

At CentCom I would sometimes joke about the reporter from Fox News who would ask before a live interview what questions I wanted him to ask, but in reality reporters from other U.S. networks did it, too. Whether their collegial manners arose out of their respect for my uniform—for the men and women engaged in battle—or were filtered down from network executives eyeing ratings, no one gave media officers like me much grief as we passed along CentCom's daily messages. In fact, the reporters seemed to hungrily swallow the stuff we served them, often without deeper inquiry—and often after abandoning the obligatory skepticism inherent in journalism. As critical as I am of the Bush administration and its disregard of the press in Iraq and elsewhere, I'm more disappointed in the U.S. media for this blatant dereliction of duty.

Norman Solomon agrees. Politicians were spontaneously selling the war as they often sell whatever actions their administration takes. "When the huge news outlets swing behind warfare," he writes in his Afterword to *War Made Easy*, "the dissent propelled by conscience is not deemed to be very newsworthy. The mass media are filled with bright lights and sizzle, with high production values and lower human values, boosting the war effort. And for many Americans, the gap between what they believe and what's on their TV sets is the distance between their truer selves and their fearful passivity."[1]

A year into the war, the *New York Times* and the *Washington Post* both apologized to the American people for their reporting leading up to the war. The *New York Times* editors released theirs, titled "The Times and Iraq," on May 26,

---

1. Norman Solomon, *War Made Easy* (John Wiley & Sons, 2006).

2004. In this unsigned editorial, the paper of record fell on its sword—sort of. "Looking back, we wish we had been more aggressive in re-examining the claims as new evidence emerged—or failed to emerge," the editors wrote. Not exactly a full-throated mea culpa.

The *Washington Post* followed suit with a front-page story in which staff media reporter Howard Kurtz chronicled the difficulty some reporters had getting their more skeptical stories the attention they deserved. "Administration assertions were on the front page," *Post* Pentagon correspondent told Kurtz. "Things that challenged the administration were on A18 on Sunday or A24 on Monday."[2]

Skepticism is more than a bullet point in a journalist's job description; it's a requirement for a democracy to work. If journalists don't crosscheck and hold the power of administrations accountable, their nation runs the risk of fascism, where all the power is held in one small office. Worse, without a dubious media, nations run the risk of going to war for the wrong reasons. The majority of U.S. journalists dutifully accepted the narrow berth allowed them. There were, however, a couple of notable exceptions at the CentCom media center.

CNN correspondent Tom Mintier always saw through the spin. He would flash a knowing smile and say, "You buried the lead." He asked tougher questions and didn't suck

---

2. "The Post on WMDs: An Inside Story," *Washington Post*, August 12, 2004.

up for access. I always thought he was a straight shooter and a good guy. I remember a conversation we had after coalition forces shelled Al Jazeera's offices in Baghdad and killed one of its correspondents, Tariq Ayyoub. That day is marked by three different incidents of journalists getting in the line of fire in Baghdad—the Palestine Hotel (where western journalists were staying), the Al Arabiya offices, and the Al Jazeera offices. U.S. forces had rolled into Baghdad that day, and a lot of bullets were flying. Al Jazeera had informed the Pentagon of its coordinates but it's unlikely that information reached pilots flying low enough over the city to look for snipers on rooftops. Ayyoub was alone on the roof, wearing a flack jacket and Kevlar helmet across from a large television camera on a tripod. To a pilot at 800 feet, he's one man in military gear on a building, surrounded by sand bags across from something on a tripod. He was killed on the spot. This was not a smart bomb.

"What are journalists saying to each other about this?" I asked Mintier.

"Journalists tend to stick together, just like soldiers stick together," he told me. Western correspondents were suspicious that Al Jazeera and another Arab network from Abu Dhabi were bombed on purpose. Al Jazeera was certain of it.

Another American who stood out from the pack at Cent-Com was AP correspondent Nicole Winfield. During one daily briefing in April 2003, Brooks deflected questions about the military's responsibility to prevent the further looting of Iraqi museums, placing the blame squarely on the people of Iraq. End of story. To Winfield, Brooks's response that the Iraqis were to blame was ridiculous. It was April 2003, and Coalition troops had just broken the city wide open. The Iraqi army and Baghdad police were nowhere to be seen. CentCom's official position was that the Iraqi citizens needed to protect their national treasures amid the chaos U.S. forces had ignited in Baghdad, but the truth was more along the lines of the military not having enough troops to protect museums, libraries, and art houses—no matter how special they were. If another nation ever invaded Washington, I imagine the Smithsonian would be the last thing on anyone's mind in the first few days. I witnessed Winfield fuming about this to Thorp, who did his level best to defend the ridiculous proposition.

Both reporters had something in common: though they were Americans, they lived abroad—Mintier in Bangkok, Winfield in Rome—and thus had been less exposed to the not-so-subtle war marketing the rest of us were being bombarded with in the United States. They weren't just reading the U.S. press—even the *New York Times* was running the Ahmad Chalabi–sanctioned WMD stories by the now-disgraced journalist Judith Miller on its front page—or just watching U.S. cable news, where CNN admitted it was clearing its military advisors with the DoD. They were open to a more skeptical, international take on the war, and less caught up in our own media's rush to approve the invasion. Of all the American journalists at CentCom working for U.S.

media companies, for the most part, only Mintier and Winfield asked the hard-hitting questions and took a different tack. I realized what the difference was: they lived outside the incubator of war as the American media had created it.

⬥

Unsavory pictures of warfare may be hard to sell, but the bigger picture is even harder to digest. As of this writing, the war in Iraq has cost more than 3,000 American lives and over 40,000 Iraqi lives (as many as 650,000 by some counts); the United States spends over half a billion dollars a day, and the final cost, in terms of the nation's reputation and the effects of the invasion on the future of the Middle East, is incalculable. None of that bears comparison with who got voted off the island last week or who will be America's Next Top Model, at least not according to the ratings of Americans' viewing habits.

On August 4, 2005, a day when fourteen marines were killed in Iraq, Greta von Susteren on Fox News chose to instead talk about old news—the May 30 disappearance of Natalee Holloway in Aruba, even though there was no news to report. Bob Costas struck a blow for all journalists that same month after refusing to be a substitute host on *Larry King Live* when he learned the topic was Holloway, whose disappearance boosted the ratings of countless cable shows.

This is the problem with our 24-hour news cycle: a genocide may well be happening right now in Darfur, but networks will spend an hour on one pretty girl that went missing months ago. In prime time you can't even get headlines on CNN Headline News because they switch to an hour-long "news feature" format. It's like MTV getting rid of music videos; I thought "headline news" meant just that. For example, I tried to find coverage about the Military Commissions Act after Bush signed it. Among other things, the bill took away the right to habeas corpus for individuals declared an enemy of the state—as well as for undocumented immigrants and Green Card holders. But instead of covering this groundbreaking diminution of civil liberties while White House spokesperson and former Fox News personality Tony Snow gave a press conference about the event, MSNBC's Rita Cosby was having a round-table interview about a recent civil lawsuit against O. J. Simpson.

My media training in the military, as well as my role as a public affairs officer and then liaison to Hollywood, may have made me cynical about the current state of the press, but I still respect its potential to inform the public and to work as a counterweight to government spin. Cable news is locked in a tragic—and often comic—battle with itself when it comes to ratings. A war works well with audiences when the United States is winning and good news is abundant—and even then falling bombs can't compete with missing blondes or celebrities in free fall. A friend of mine who is stationed in Iraq sent me an e-mail asking, "Do they even remember we're here?"

In a rare one-on-one interview on June 8, 2005, Fox News's Neil Cavuto, after giving Bush easy swings on the topic of the day—Social Security reform, which was stalling on Capitol Hill—asked the commander-in-chief about the effects of Michael Jackson's latest problems with accusations of pedophilia. "I mean, his trial and his ongoing saga has gripped the nation for the past four-and-a-half, five months as you've been on this campaign," Cavuto observed, even plugging an upcoming Fox News feature on the Jackson saga. The question caused some laughter in the room, and Cavuto certainly meant no disrespect: "I know this is a little outlandish, Mr. President—"

"No," Bush assured him, "that's all right, Neil."

Mollified, Cavuto continued. "Do you think that the focus on Michael Jackson has hurt you?"

"I have no idea," said Bush. "I don't spend a lot of time trying to figure out, you know, the viewing of American TV audiences. I do know what my job is, and there's a serious problem with Social Security. . . ."

As he said, Bush may know what his job is, but Cavuto failed in his: in the long, sit-down interview with the president, Cavuto did not use the time to press the president on the situation in Iraq, or on what, if any, new thinking there might be in the White House on how to resolve it. As a matter of fact, Cavuto, one of Fox News's star hosts, didn't ask a single question about Iraq, where 23 Marines, 54 soldiers, 4 airmen, 1 sailor, and 1 DoD Army civilian had been killed in the previous 30 days, not to mention the uncounted dead on the other side and those caught in the middle. (Cavuto was less kind when he interviewed me on November 24, 2004, and insinuated that my appreciation for Al Jazeera extended to Al Qaeda. "You're friends with Al Jazeera and they're friends with Al Qaeda, aren't you comforting the enemy?" For an instant, I considered leaping across his desk, but decided it would be bad for my message of understanding and mutual tolerance.)

Since going to work for Al Jazeera English and reporting on military spin and its media targets, I have unearthed some old footage of myself supplying Fox News with the message of the day. I'm defending reports of civilian casualties in Iraq and saying things like, "America is such a benevolent nation but look at what the enemy is doing: fighting us in civilian clothes, so that innocent people become the target." I hit my lines and, in retrospect, it's pretty embarrassing—but I was doing my job. The question is if the American media remembers what *its* job is.

At CentCom, Jim mostly preferred to stay behind the cameras but in one case, Kelly O'Donnell, an NBC reporter, landed an interview for the *Today Show* after the statue of Saddam was toppled in Baghdad. O'Donnell was getting ready for the stand-up interview as they both watched images of U.S. tanks driving through the city on a monitor off camera.

"A lot of young men and women died to make this moment happen," Jim says, before adding, "a lot of reporters too." Clearly in his mind, the reporters were helping "to make this happen." O'Donnell knowingly nods her head in agreement. (I somehow don't think he was referring to Ayyoub.)

When the interview went live, O'Donnell asked Jim the tough questions—"What are the most striking images you've seen thus far?"—allowing him to do his thing. "Anytime you see men, women and children celebrating. . . ."

When they went off the air, while Jim unhooked his mike, O'Donnell thanked him profusely. "You did great," she said repeating it. "You did great."

He could have said the same to her.

CHAPTER FOUR
"JUST WALK AWAY"

In April 2003 I was ordered by Thorp to give Abdullah Schleifer, the Washington bureau chief for Al Arabiya, an interview for his online journal about transnational broadcasting. This was, in fact, how I came to know the eclectic Schleifer. Thorp's hectic schedule simply didn't allow him to engage in Schleifer's style of reporting, long conversations. He also asked if one of his graduate students at the American University in Cairo could film the interview. Thorp, keeping the conversation short, agreed, and Schleifer invited Jehane Noujaim and Hani Salama to film the interview. Noujaim and Salama were allowed to hang around the media center for another couple of weeks. They were making a film about Al Jazeera, and it appeared to me to be the lowest-budget film imaginable. Their crew consisted of just the two of them, and they were sleeping on someone's couch. (I later learned that they weren't *just* college students; Noujaim already had directed the excellent documentary *Startup.com*, and Salama had made a couple of indie films in Egypt.)

I didn't give Noujaim and Salama's film a shot in hell, but I didn't mind them tagging along either. I was probably more cynical than most about these matters because I lived in Los Angeles, where every bar and restaurant is full of directors and actors who happen to be waiting tables there, and most of their projects never see the white of the big screen.

One day Noujaim and Salama brought Hassan Ibrahim, a producer for Al Jazeera, to meet me at CentCom. Hassan was a central character of their project, and they filmed our forty-five-minute conversation. Hassan is a mountain of a man—if the floor isn't solid, you can hear, if not feel, the rattle of his footsteps approaching from afar; and he's blessed with a proportionately oversized charm. Even so, most of Hassan's points were hostile, but I specialized in such conversations and recognized them as standard-issue anti-Americanisms to which I tried to answer as honestly as possible, searching for a place in the conversation where we could agree, or at least a place where one of us didn't have to be wrong for the other to be right. I listened to his side of the story and gave him all the information I had. Our talk was forgotten quickly as I prepped for the next one—it was all in a day's work.

One conversation that occurred during Noujaim's and Salama's two-week stint at CentCom will never slip into the abyss of forgotten memories. Salama is a tall, good-looking Egyptian who, after working in front of the camera in a number of Arab films, has now become a documentary filmmaker. At the time that I met Salama in 2003, he had never visited the United States and was filled with the same prejudices as many other Arabs.

Salama asked me, "Can I talk to you off-camera?" We went into a little side office and he said, "Do you really believe what you are saying about America? Isn't it lacking in any real cultural value? From here it appears to be all Coke and fries and corporate logos. We Arabs have a deep cultural history that is very important to us. What if we don't want to become immersed in your disposable culture? How can you be a spiritual Muslim in your materialistic country?"

He listened closely to me when I defended America in my debate with Hassan, and when I explained what I thought was great about the United States.

"In America no one will force you to be a pious Muslim," I told him, "yet you have the freedom to be the most pious Muslim in the world." Again, the "greater jihad" refers to the personal battle we all have in overcoming the worst parts of ourselves. I asked Salama, "If you really want to conquer your greater jihad, is it better to do so because the government is forcing you? Or because you have chosen freely to embark on that struggle?"

A few days later I saw Noujaim, the director, interviewing Salama on camera. He didn't notice me watching them. He said, "You know, I think all these bad things about America—but when I hear Lieutenant Josh talking about the United States, I want to see it for myself. I want to experience the America he describes." I reflect back on few occasions in my life with more pride than that single stolen moment.

Salama finally traveled to the United States when *Control Room* was released. He visited New York and didn't want to leave. "I can see now in America how you could not care as much about what's going on in the rest of the world," he told me at the time. "I'm so busy here, essentially trying to fulfill my own dreams. I play guitar, I'm trying to make music, I'm doing these films—I'm just so wrapped up in this that I've kind of forgotten what is going on in the rest of the world."

Within a matter of days after my conversations with Hassan and Salama, Baghdad fell, and within a few weeks of that CentCom's Qatar media operations were disbanded. Media operations for OIF transferred to what would become the Green Zone, a heavily fortified area of downtown Baghdad from where L. Paul Bremer of the Coalition Provisional Authority (CPA) would rule occupied Iraq for the next year.

I volunteered to go to Baghdad and did so for a short trip in April 2003 to help host Iraq's first constitutional convention. These were heady times compared to what was to come. Shia, Sunni, Kurds, ex-patriots, and secular leaders all came together to discuss how a constitution should be written. A fleeting glimmer of hope hung in the air.

After six months in the Middle East, my tour at CentCom ended on July 3, 2003. My wife Paige and I took a week off before returning to Los Angeles to share my first Independence Day as a war veteran in New York City.

Aside from the well-documented difficulties of transitioning from war abroad to peace at home, I experienced one unanticipated and curious effect. After many months of staring at nothing but desert brown buildings on desert brown sand, my vision had been deprived of almost all colors. The neon buzz of the Big Apple was like an overdose of adrenalin to my senses, yet my mind was trapped half a world away, in a place where everything, every day, seemed of vital importance. I had lost my appetite for my position in Los Angeles, which seemed trivial and insignificant after my return, and before long I dreamed of another tour in the Middle East where my service would really mean something again.

I was obsessed with all the news pouring in from the front, particularly with the idea that our military was making a huge mistake with Al Jazeera. But as a lieutenant (soon to be a captain) I could do little. At the time, I was the only person in the world who had been inside the Pentagon, the Bush administration (through Jim), and Al Jazeera. But I felt that my unique vantage point didn't add up to much if no one cared to hear what I thought. Nonetheless I had wanted to stay in the Corps and fight the good fight: resist the trend toward the role of public affairs officers becoming less about being constitutional watchdogs insuring a transparent military for the public good, and more about being PR spokespeople promoting the whims of politicians.

After being home for seven months, on Monday morning, February 2, 2004, I was sitting at my desk in Hollywood, hating my vapid job, when I picked up a message on my answering machine. "I just saw your movie at Sundance," the stranger said, "and I wanted to say thanks." An anonymous voice on an answering machine had just warned me that my life was forever changed, whether I realized it or not.

During my tour in Hollywood I had represented the Marine Corps in a few projects and, seemingly, like everyone else in town, had even acted in a few independent movies. Still, I couldn't imagine which of them my mystery caller was referring to. So I Googled my name and up popped *Control Room*, a film I'd never heard of, and numerous links to websites that discussed the film, particularly my role in it. After reading several blogs, I figured it out: Noujaim and Salama's project on Al Jazeera made it.

As I surfed from one website to the next featuring debates about *me*, I started to panic a bit; it was so bizarre. After a few calls, I was able to contact Noujaim. A year had passed since I last saw her at CentCom. About a month later, a couple of publicists came to my office with a VHS copy of the film.

Paige and I, along with a couple of friends, watched what for me felt more like a home movie than a film. I could remember what was around every corner the viewer couldn't see. I recalled every nameless person that passed through the background of every scene. It was surreal for Paige, too; video was laid over all the stories I had shared with her about the media center and its odd batch of characters.

Only later did I find out I wasn't supposed to be a main character in the film. I didn't sign a release or give my contact information. They expected me to remain a nameless spokesperson who their character, Hassan, interacted with. But things changed when the original editor for *Control Room* left the project, and Julia Bacha stepped in.

Bacha, a Brazilian, had graduated in 2003 from Columbia University after studying Farsi and Persian culture and had remained in New York City while awaiting approval for her visa to Iran, where she planned to attend the University of Tehran for her master's degree. She was introduced to Noujaim by a mutual friend, and Bacha was brought on as an advisor to the film and joined Jehane and crew in Cairo. Bacha fell in love with the concept, and shortly after her arrival the original editor had to leave the project. Bacha, with no editing experience, jumped at the opportunity to fill the gap. Armed with a book on Final Cut Pro, the favorite editing program of independent filmmakers, Bacha set to work so obsessively her eyes swelled and she had to see a doctor. Bacha was assigned to the scenes where I appeared, and she decided with Noujaim to edit my conversation with Hassan into segments and to use them as a bridging device for the rest of the film, with the war raging in the background. I emerged from the editing-room floor as a central character in *Control Room*, someone an American audience could relate to: a Marine with a conscience.

My debate with Hassan presented a sort of litmus test for the audience. Conservatives come away saying, "Josh never gave up his principles and represented us well." Liberals walk away saying, "Josh really saw things differently by the end. He was a thoughtful and honest spokesperson."

One of the scenes that garnered the most attention concerned the dead. At one point in the documentary, Al Jazeera showed the infamous images of killed and captured U.S. soldiers from PFC Jessica Lynch's squad. Dead American soldiers were lying uncovered on a cold concrete floor with their blood flowing down a drain. Two Iraqi guards were laughing and smoking cigarettes while positioning their bodies for the camera.

I was sickened. On a bank of televisions mounted to the wall, one screen was always on Al Jazeera. When it broadcast the video of the captured U.S. soldiers, all eyes were on it. Even though Al Jazeera's anchor apologized before broadcasting the images, the coalition forces were not buying the network's excuse that the footage was aired "in the interest of objectivity." Rumsfeld said, "It's a violation of the Geneva Convention for the Iraqis to be showing prisoners of war in a humiliating manner." And British Prime Minister Tony Blair agreed with him.

I felt the angry looks of my peers as they saw the video shown repeatedly on the network I championed. It was a lonely walk to my tent in the warehouse that night. As I lay in my bunk thinking about the video, I remembered some footage I had seen the night before while I was in the Al Jazeera office surrounded by its Arab employees. Al Jazeera was showing footage of bloodied and mangled Iraqis being rushed to a hospital after a bombing in Basra. The scenes, just as gory as the footage of fallen U.S. soldiers, should have been equally upsetting, but they hadn't been. This was an awakening for me.

Control Room captured me in a moment of self-reflection, remembering that incident. "I just saw people on the other side," I said, "and those people in the Al Jazeera offices must have felt the way I was feeling that night, and it upset me on a profound level that I wasn't bothered as much the night before. It makes me hate war. . . . But it doesn't make me believe that we're in a world that can live without war yet."

Viewers come away from the film thinking that over the course of the war I evolve from war supporter to skeptic. Few realize that most of the footage on me stems from a single, very well-edited conversation. During that conversation we touched on complex ideas, and Noujaim and Bacha found sufficient material to represent an arc of personal growth. At one point I actually walk away from the conversation with Hassan and say, "You will not convince me that we are not here for the good of the Iraqi people." Later in the conversation I admit that I can understand how some would see the United States as occupiers. I was trying to hold on to the idea that the invasion was serving a greater good while acknowledging that others would see the invasion as naked aggression. Noujaim and Bacha were following lesson number one in Hollywood script writing: your hero must have an arc, he can't start off a great guy and end up a great guy. He's got to change and that's why people fall in love with him.

The power of transformation is not just a Hollywood secret; it's found at the heart of Marine Corps recruitment as well. While the other military services sell benefits, a Marine Corps commercial will never talk about job perks, whether they're educational, financial, or otherwise. The Army says, *We'll give you money;* the Navy says, *You'll see the world;* the Air Force says, *We'll give you a job.* Yet the Army often struggles to make their recruitment quotas while the Marines never miss theirs. Why? Because the Marine Corps sells transformation: *We'll change you into something better than what you are now.* The Corps powerfully taps into the primal desire for betterment that exists in all of us. Noujaim and Bacha gave my character in the movie that arc of transformation for audiences worldwide to see.

Control Room hit theaters right in the middle of the Abu Ghraib scandal; the film's debut was May 21, 2004, at New York's Film Forum (a run that broke all box office records for that theater). Lots of people bought their movie tickets thinking the military was chock full of ignorant, xenophobic rapists, and abusers from West Virginia like Army Specialist

Charles Graner and Private Lynndie England. Early in the film I'm shown delivering hard on-message lines—the war according to Rumsfeld. Sitting in the audience of the premiere I could sense audience members jeering at me and thinking, *He's the bad guy.* This notion begins to dissolve, though, during the scene where I admit how deeply troubled I had been that Al Jazeera's footage of Iraqi dead—those the United States had come to liberate—hadn't bothered me as much as the images of our dead.

The thread is cleverly edited. Noujaim and Bacha cut to a shot of Iraqi dead, and for most people it passes with only mild discomfort because we've seen a lot of that kind of carnage. But then, when the audience sees U.S. soldiers on the ground, they see their American troops, their sons and daughters bleeding out on a foreign floor. That's when it registers, and they go through a transition similar to my own at the time: why, only moments before, had they not been as affected by the Iraqi dead and wounded? The audience begins to relate.

The filmmakers made me appear like someone who, while never giving up what he believed in, really did want to understand the other side and do the right thing. I like to think it's an accurate portrayal. I can understand that for audiences who were grappling with their own mixed emotions about the war—who supported the invasion but not the occupation, or who had sympathy for the troops but not the arrogant leaders who sent them—I may have been someone they found hope in.

I think the military could have used *Control Room* to counterbalance the terrible Abu Ghraib pictures that had just
been published as an example of how things can go right in
the military. Columnist Frank Rich, no fan of the military,
wrote a piece in the *New York Times* on May 16, 2004, com-
paring me and Private England as the best and worst, respectively, of what the military had to offer. He suggested
that I could have been used as a voice of understanding.
The American public needed someone to help them understand, but the Pentagon decided to go a different route with
my story, particularly after an interview I gave to the *Village
Voice* for a story appeared on May 11, 2004, ten days before
the film's premiere.

In the interview I said, "I think it should all be shown, the
dead on both sides. In America, war isn't hell, we don't see
blood, we don't see suffering. All we see is patriotism, and we
support the troops. It's almost like war has some brand marketing here. Al Jazeera shows it all. It turns your stomach,
and you remember there's something wrong with war."

I believe Marines are supposed to be reluctant warriors
with an intimate disdain for war. Yet people within the Pentagon thought my quote had gone too far, that I had gone outside of my lane. To the senior leadership in Marine Corps
public affairs, my comments sounded like criticism of *the* war,
rather than criticism of *all* war. Amid the Abu Ghraib scan-

dal, the Pentagon had a guy in uniform who could have put a better face on the military and the war, yet they turned against me. I always chuckle when I think of Jon Stewart's observation that I wasn't "dickish" enough for them. I don't know about that but I do believe the Pentagon missed a strategic opportunity with my situation.

Instead, they accused me of vying for my fifteen minutes of fame in a project my current chain of command did not support. Some seemed not to believe me when I told them I had been ordered to cooperate with the makers of *Control Room*; I think they suspected that I had gone native over there and was cooperating with Arab filmmakers on my own initiative. They called to confirm my story with CentCom, but like I had, the men and women with whom I had served in our desert media center had all dispersed and returned to other jobs. Even the warehouse had been closed down and converted into an R&R facility for troops who needed a break from the frontlines.

So there I was in New York in May 2004, just hours away from *Control Room*'s theatrical premiere and the Marines at the Pentagon are getting madder and madder, leaving messages on my cell phone questioning my loyalty, and demanding proof that I was acting under orders when I appeared in the film. The only person who could really save my reputation in the eyes of the Pentagon was Thorp, the very man who had ordered me to allow Noujaim and Salama to follow me at CentCom. Clearly, I needed to get in touch with Thorp as soon as possible.

Just days earlier I had picked up the *New York Times* and the front page pictured Rumsfeld and General Richard Myers, Joint Chiefs of Staff, striding across the grounds of Abu Ghraib, where they had just made a surprise visit. And behind them in the back of the photograph, was my alibi-in-the-flesh, Thorp. The only person who could explain why I had participated in *Control Room* was at this very moment in Abu Ghraib—a media advisor dealing with the biggest media story of the moment. My fate was sealed; the order was issued: "You may not speak to the press. If a reporter puts a microphone in your face," the Pentagon officer summed it up with a command as precise as it was prescient, "just walk away."

While they didn't stop me from attending the film's premiere—on my own time and out of uniform—they silenced me by enjoining me not to speak to the press. They turned down media requests for interviews with me, including a one-on-one with NPR's Terry Gross. The major who made the call turned to a captain I know and said, "What the hell is *Fresh Air*, anyway?"

Until the Pentagon censored me, all the coverage of *Control Room* was nestled deep within newspapers in the entertainment section. But in a classic PR bungle, the Pentagon's "no comment" added fuel to a slow-burning fire. The story was propelled from E–1, the entertainment section, to A–1, the front page.

I didn't want the story to grow, but I did want to speak about it. As an American citizen, it felt bizarre that the government was restricting me from doing something legal and constitutional. It felt wrong: what I had to say wasn't classified or anti-military, even if the administration didn't like it.

Yet, I kept to my work. And as I told a group of military officers at Naval Base Coronado in San Diego after they watched *Control Room*, "You have to engage the media. You can't say one thing in the foreign press and another in the States. The truth will always come out and once you lose your integrity there's no getting it back." The officers in attendance mostly outranked me, and I knew this was going to be a tough crowd even before I arrived at the auditorium. (Little did I know how often I would end up facing similar crowds with an even more controversial message in my new life to come. Nor did I know that a new life was just over the horizon.)

As I waited to address this group, I got a cell phone call that staggered me. A friend of mine named Major Terry Thomas excitedly asked, "Have you seen the front page of the *LA Times*? Listen to this." And then he read the day's front-page story—about me.

The paper had requested an interview with me from my chain of command at the Pentagon, but the request was turned down, which was the point of the story. The article included a number of positive comments about me from military officers and high-level political people, and a few quotes from my former boss at Miramar, Lieutenant Colonel Kay, who was at HQMC. Kay told the reporter,

"He did a few interviews that indicated that he might not know what his lane is."

Terry read me the whole story and said, "Dude, you're screwed!" I hung up the phone and walked into the crowd of senior military officers who were waiting to hear me speak about the Arab press. The timing of events couldn't have been more bizarre. I started the speech by saying, "This is probably the last time I'll speak in public in uniform."

The Pentagon strayed from its lane when my superiors asked me to silence Paige. On her own accord, she had spoken to the press a couple of times, once to Salon.com, and once to the *Fort Worth Star Telegraph*. Paige felt the reporter for the latter paper had an agenda and, as it turned out, the reporter cherry-picked her answers. After that, Paige decided not to talk to the press anymore. That same reporter also spoke with my dad, unbeknownst to me or to him. The man did not identify himself as a reporter on a story, so Dad simply thought the man was interested in me because of the movie and talked openly to the reporter about how I had been a "special" kid.

Paige's criticism of the way the military was handling the controversy, along with my father's quotes in the press, made the brass even angrier. I received an e-mail from Kay that said, "Call off your back channel media campaign." It was hurtful—he should have given me the benefit of the doubt. They assumed the worst of my family and me and asked me to do things that were beyond their authority, like telling my family not to talk to whoever they wanted to speak to. That's when I realized I needed to resign. The organization I had been so loyal to for so long was, in the end, less than loyal to me.

I easily separated the methods of the current administration from the Marine Corps. In fourteen years I had served under five administrations: Bush, father and son, for three terms, and Clinton for two terms. Like every other American, I did not always agree with their politics. I served the United States, not the specific administration.

The Marine Corps, however, was sacred in my heart, and I loved the institution. I was heartbroken that the Corps assumed the worst of me. Years before, as a second lieutenant at Miramar in San Diego, I had worked directly for Kay—he knew me and should have known better.

I submitted my resignation in August 2004—it's an official form that didn't require me to spell out my reasons. I didn't have to resign; I could have continued to have a career with the Marines, maybe even in a consulate or embassy abroad as a foreign area officer. On my last day, October 14, 2004, I worked alone in the office. Headquarters didn't call; the Pentagon didn't call. I had given the day off to my Marines, so no one said farewell. At the end of the day, after fourteen years to the week of active duty in the Marine Corps, I left my key on the desk and shut the door behind me.

It wasn't only the end of my career. I had joined the Marines at seventeen. For my entire adult life, I had been in the Corps; I had been a Marine. I shed the uniform, but not the purpose.

I came out of that office convinced I had an obligation. I knew something was wrong with America—our media was leading us down the wrong path; the administration was wrong about Al Jazeera; and, most important, the way the government was dealing with the Arab network was dangerous. When I returned from Doha, I didn't have a platform on which to say it. Now, I had the opportunity to speak my mind, and the public affairs officers in the Pentagon had unwittingly built the platform for me.

Life can open itself up to you, but you have to be available when it does. My appearance in *Control Room* and its fallout represented just such an opportunity. It was a perfect convergence of life and a person who was ready, as the Corps taught, to do the right thing.

I left the Marine Corps with the same sense of civic responsibility I had when I joined. My loyalty extended beyond the Marine Corps: it was to America and to the values I believe my country is supposed to stand for. I had no job, no prospects, and no savings. I had been told I would get six months of transitional health care, and the day I left I found out that wasn't true. But there was something I had to do. I had to go on Gross's *Fresh Air*, on *Nightline*, on the *O'Reilly Factor*, because I knew those shows had access to the people I had to reach.

I spoke on campuses and in front of private groups; any place that would have me. I didn't know enough at first to ask for an honorarium. My only requirement was that they had to fly Paige with me. We'd spent too much time apart, and I have no interest in being away from her if I can help it. She was the one going over our finances and worrying because our savings—otherwise known as a second mortgage—were drying up.

I finally was offered a job with a Houston PR firm, and was in the process of accepting it when Paul Gibbs, Al Jazeera English's newly hired director of programming, called. He had just seen *Control Room*, and he wanted to know if I would come to Washington to pilot a show for the new English-language network of Al Jazeera, which at the time had just a handful of employees.

When I told my family Al Jazeera had offered me a job, their reaction was, "Whoa, Josh. Al Jazeera. You know, you may never work again." And although I knew this might be true, I couldn't imagine passing up this opportunity to practice what I had preached for months. I had been out there saying we don't understand the Arab press, and the way we deal with it is dangerous. Now that I was being offered a chance to follow up on what I had challenged Bill O'Reilly and all the media to reconsider, was I going to be a coward and not take that opportunity? For better or for worse I had to do it.

Paige and I moved to Washington in August 2005, a year after I left the Marine Corps. When the news of my new job broke, I was branded the new face of Al Jazeera by the American press.

For some, the choice to make myself such an obvious target in these partisan times might seem insane: I was going out of the frying pan and into the fire. But in the simple moral maxim the Marine Corps teaches—do the right thing, for the right reason—no exception exists that says: unless there's criticism or risk. Damn the consequences.

I work as a military correspondent for Al Jazeera English, part correspondent and part military analyst. Because I'm in programming as opposed to news, I shoot long-form pieces either as stand-alone specials or for use in any one of our current affairs shows. For my part, though, I view my role there as that of cultural ambassador. I hope to represent the best of what America stands for. I want to see myself as a cultural bridge. Many Americans don't understand the rest of the world, and the rest of the world often doesn't understand America: its values, its heritage, its opportunities. A bridge is a two-way street, and just as we can expose and export the elements about our society that we hold dear, we need to be open ourselves to other cultures and experiences. Openness will help us to see something more than danger out there in the world.

Media are meant to be like a window through which we can perceive the world. Unfortunately, the media too often works like a mirror, with people looking into it and seeing but a reflection of themselves, and, perhaps, a distorted view of the world beyond. This is true of the Arab media as well as of our own; the mirror has two sides and we need to see past our own images and preconceptions in order to find the truth. If I can show the Arab world that we in the United States are capable of questioning and challenging ourselves, and that people here care about more than just themselves, I will have served some higher purpose.

Surprisingly, the reaction of the military to my new mission, and to my job with Al Jazeera, has not been as negative as one might have expected. Given the wave of publicity about my resignation (the front-page headline in the *Los Angeles Times* read: "Marine Lands in Film, Collides with Superiors") and the headlines I made when I took my latest job (*USA Today* reported: "Media Glare Is On Former Marine As He Joins Ranks of Al Jazeera"), you might think I'd be persona non grata, even out of uniform.

And while the Marine Corps reaped a lot of bad press for muzzling me—not to mention their desire to quiet my wife and family—when I spoke my mind about the war in Iraq and the politicization of the Pentagon, the military is not monolithic; within its ranks are commanders who are very progressive and open to my views, just as there are service members who consider my beliefs traitorous. Rest assured, a debate goes on within the military as pitched as any you'll find on the campuses or in the town halls of America. Since I resigned my commission, leaders of both camps have sought me out to engage in this discussion, and I've been asked back to speak at numerous military events. My alma mater DIN-FOS, for one, has invited me to speak to classes of public affairs officers. I've also spoken at West Point half a dozen times since I quit, and I'll have been there again by the time you read this.

Military audiences can be tough crowds. I'm always asked, "If things were so wrong with the military, why did you get out instead of staying in and correcting the system?" But I had been limited and silenced, just as the media said. When I got out, I eagerly participated in the widespread debate going on about *me*—on the web and the radio, in newspapers and on television. I didn't get out and then start wondering about what I could do to contribute to this discussion; I got out because I felt I could affect change and be a positive influence. I needed to say some things that I couldn't say in uniform, so I had to give my uniform back.

During a symposium on war and media held at West Point in the spring of 2006, I participated in a panel with Greg Palkot (a Fox News reporter who had been embedded with the Marines in Iraq), Jane Arraf (the former CNN Baghdad bureau chief), and Kevin Sites (the Hot Zone reporter from Yahoo News). We were appearing in an auditorium before about a thousand cadets, mostly graduating seniors. The format was simple: each reporter brought a sample of their war reporting, stuff from when they were on the scene in Iraq, and then talked about it. Sites, who works as a sort of one-man band online, putting up still photos and videos of hot spots he's visited on his blog, showed the well-known footage he captured of a Marine shooting an unarmed man in a mosque, along with some other footage to put the first one in context.

Arraf, who was then an adjunct senior fellow at the Council of Foreign Relations, drew on her experience as one of the few Arabic-speaking television reporters in Iraq and as her time as chief of CNN's Baghdad bureau. Palkot showed a clip about a squad that had been ambushed going into a house in Fallujah and later got their revenge. He had shown up right about when the squad was going in to make sure "these terrorists got theirs" so his story had that *ooh-rah* feel to it. Seeing Marines firing into the building where the insurgents were positioned got the crowd going. Rounds exploded; dirt flew; Palkot said something to the effect of making sure those terrorists wouldn't kill again; and everyone cheered.

I showed the scene from *Control Room* of PFC Lynch's squad after some of them had been captured and killed by the Iraqis; it had a notably different feel than the Fox clip. An Iraqi child waits in the ER with stitches all over his face. Dead U.S. soldiers lie on a cement floor. Then I reflect on the effect the footage had on me compared to how I felt earlier seeing dead Iraqis.

When I speak in public I usually shoot from the hip. I've done it so many times I know which jokes hit and which ones don't on certain audiences, and most of the time people already know something about me going in. Some already have made up their minds. This panel's format only allowed for a short introduction—perilously insufficient time to explain to a group of service members and former peers why my actions, which might be perceived by them as traitorous or treasonous, were neither.

I simply had time to offer, "I served as a captain in the Marine Corps. Now I work for Al Jazeera. I look forward to your comments and especially your questions about both the clip and my change of career."

Rumsfeld had just gone to the Council of Foreign Relations on February 17, 2006, and said for the first time that Iraq was spinning out of control. He said the Pentagon didn't fully understand the information age yet: "For the most part, the U.S. government still functions as a five and dime store in the e-Bay age." Enemies of America were utilizing new Internet, cell phone, and video technologies far more efficiently than the U.S. military. By posting videos of sniper attacks on blogs, hosting web pages with messages encrypted in the images, and spreading viral videos by cell phone, for example, the insurgents and terrorists were sailing past the bureaucratic Pentagon and its bloated communications experts.

Rumsfeld's speech was delivered not long after one of the Shia's most holy mosques in Samarra was bombed, igniting sectarian violence and the beginnings of a civil war. Those who had proclaimed that the U.S. military would be welcomed with flowers were starting to look for someone to blame.

I was surprised that the cadets' hostility that day was not directed at me as I had expected (they hadn't seen Al Jazeera, and I doubt many of them had seen *Control Room*), but against the U.S. media. For the first time while speaking to the military I got the sense they felt the war was going downhill. And it was the U.S. media's fault—not the Arab media. "This thing is starting to slip from us, this war could go bad," cadets said, "and it's the media's fault. Every day the media shows negative story after negative story from Iraq. Why don't you show the *good* stories about Iraq?"

I was witnessing what often happens when wars go on longer than people expect them to: images from the front-lines start affecting the populace negatively and finally turns it against the war—and then the military turns against the media. When the tides started to turn against U.S. forces in Iraq, the military wanted the media to show positive stories, not just the bad stuff. For the American people to maintain the will to persevere, they need to have a sense that progress is being made, that the sacrifices are worth it.

As a result, Arraf received far tougher questions than I did. She was all but accused of only giving people the bad news, while Palkot was applauded as a member of their team: if a line in the sand had been drawn, his network was on their side.

After a relatively brief Q&A session, we were surrounded by cadets asking us individual questions, but the largest crowd gathered around a television in the corner to watch the National Collegiate Athletic Association (NCAA), men's basketball tournament. We then moved to a bar on campus called Thirsty's, where we talked and answered questions until closing time.

During the introductions I had been looking out over this sea of faces—most of them cadets—and identified a Marine officer sitting in front (probably an instructor on some kind of exchange program) as someone most likely to challenge me. We have a tendency to eat our own; that's how we say it in the Marine Corps. But I didn't hear a word from him. Instead, I got an e-mail some time later from a sergeant cadet in attendance who said, "I was ready to attack you for working for Al Jazeera, but as it turns out my ignorance and lack of knowledge about the network distorted my view of reality. I think the network's idea to transmit from different global positions with different perspectives has the possibility to revolutionize media. . . . I look forward to using Al Jazeera English as my primary source of cable news." Unfortunately, unless the cadet is stationed overseas he's still waiting. At the time of this writing, Al Jazeera English is not distributed in the United States except over the Internet (I discuss the reasons for this in chapter eight).

I believe my story is part of a larger calling: internationally, we've moved into the media age; a huge war is being waged over the airwaves and the United States doesn't even seem to be on the battlefield—it's caught in the echo chamber on its own home turf. It's time to really start engaging.

Family portrait taken in Lone Star, Texas, 2005. Back row, left to right: Paige and Scott (my brother-in-law). Middle row, left to right: Me, Mom, Dad, D'Lee (my sister). Front row, left to right: Luke, Noah (D'Lee's oldest son), Hannah (D'Lee's daughter) and Eli (D'Lee's youngest son).

Matt Worrell (on right) and me at Graduation Festivities, May 1990.

In dress blues, standing in front of the Hollywood sign. This photo was taken while I was working in Los Angeles as a Motion Picture and Television Liaison, December 2002.

(left) *Filming for a story on North Dakota's declining population, May 2006.*

(below) *Standing in front of CentCom's warehouse during Operation Iraqi Freedom, 2003.*

Screen-shot of a television in our CentCom office as I was being interviewed on Al Jazeera, Doha, Qatar, 2003.

His Highness the Emir of Qatar, Sheikh Hamad bin Khalifa Al Thani, Elizabeth Filippouli, and me in the reddish glow of the Al Jazeera English newsroom on November 1, 2006, two weeks before launch.

Al Jazeera English employees on launch day, November 15, 2006. I'm on the television.

CHAPTER FIVE
AL JAZEERA TAKES ON THE ARAB WORLD

[*Author's note: The quotes in this chapter, from Al Jazeera watchers Lawrence Pintak, Adel Iskandar, and Marc Lynch, were taken from taped phone interviews conducted in November 2006.*]

Qatar, a tiny peninsular nation, sits on the world's second largest natural gas reserve, but its social progressiveness compared to the rest of the region is regarded by many as its greatest asset. After seizing power of Qatar from his father in

1995, Sheikh Hamad bin Khalifa Al Thani, the Emir of Qatar, implemented unparalleled governmental reform. He oversaw the composition of a constitution and formation of an elected body known as the Municipal Council. Women were given the right to vote, work, drive, and even hold government offices. Qatar's Minister of Education, Sheikha Al Mahmoud, who also sits on Al Jazeera's board, represents the sort of powerful, educated women who have risen to positions of prominence since the new Emir took power.

Women make up two-thirds of the student body at the University of Qatar, and the Emir's wife, Sheikha Moza, spends much of her time promoting both education and women's rights in the country. The Emir, who went to school in London, believes strongly in the power of an educated population, and offers free education to Qatari citizens from kindergarten through university. Under his government, American universities such as Carnegie Mellon, Texas A&M, and Georgetown have opened campuses in Qatar's Education City. This cultural openness even encompasses religion, as Qatar hosts an annual interfaith conference that includes Christians, Muslims, and Jews, an unheard-of occurrence in the region.

In November 1996, the Emir founded a new satellite television channel, Al Jazeera, building from the remnants of the short-lived Arabic version of the BBC World Service news, a joint Saudi-BBC venture that unraveled because of cultural and ethical differences. In 1996, when the BBC network aired an interview with prominent Saudi dissident

Muhammad Al Mas'ari against the objections of the Saudi royal family, a mysterious blackout ended the transmission. More problems arose later that same year, when Arabic BBC wanted to run a documentary criticizing Saudi-style justice—floggings and decapitations. The Saudi financiers pulled the plug on the network, replacing Arabic BBC on the satellite with the Disney Channel.

When Arabic BBC shut down, the Middle East—a region with no real free press—had a surplus of unemployed, BBC-trained Arab reporters and producers. The Emir recognized an opportunity and hired about 120 of them to launch a new station. At the time, Arab media was largely state run and censored—the mouthpiece of whatever government held power. Even Qatar's own Ministry of Information existed largely to control and censor the existing media in the country. But the new Emir envisioned a different kind of network: the first Arab free press in the Middle East.

In 1996, after an attempt to overthrow the Emir was foiled, Al Jazeera broadcast the trial of the would-be usurpers. This was unique, even though a cynic might argue that it behooves a king to show his people what happens to those who plot against him. But this was no show trial; the defense claimed the suspects had been tortured, and a witness from Amnesty International decried Qatar's system of justice, all on live television.

Finally, the Emir abolished the Ministry of Information in 1998, giving Al Jazeera's reporters and producers greater freedom and license to ask tough questions and challenge conventional wisdom, a practice the ministry once made illegal and dangerous. Even the last of the skeptics had to admit that the Emir's reforms signified a new era under the Arab sun.

Following a policy unprecedented in the region, Al Jazeera lays all facts and opinions on the table. By publicly challenging their politics and policies, the network has angered the royal family of Saudi Arabia, the Palestinian Authority, the clerics of Iran, and the secular government of Egypt, among many others.

Bahrain accused Al Jazeera of harboring pro-Israeli and anti-Bahrainian sentiments in 2002 and kicked the station out of the country. Algeria jailed Al Jazeera journalists in 2004 and froze the network's ability to broadcast from within its borders after the reporters criticized the Algerian government and military leadership. The channel was accused of inciting protests in Iran in 2005. Al Jazeera has fared no better in Saudi Arabia, where the network has been accused of "serving poison on a golden platter." Jordan, Kuwait, Sudan, and Tunisia have all expelled the network at one time.

Because Al Jazeera broadcasts some of bin Laden's tapes, the U.S. government considers the network the mouthpiece of Al Qaeda, while the terrorist organization itself—together with many Islamic nations—accuses Al Jazeera of being a shill for the Zionists. Before Hamas came to power, its leaders used Al Jazeera to make their case to a larger Arab audience—and sometimes to take a jab at the Palestinian Authority. A fact shocking to most Arab countries is that Al

Jazeera broadcast Israelis defending their cause during the *intifadas*. Israeli officials appear regularly on Al Jazeera, giving interviews in Hebrew, English, and Arabic.

Ironically, Israel is about the only country in the Middle East that *hasn't* kicked out Al Jazeera's reporters. According to a 2006 *Foreign Policy* article by Al Jazeera chronicler Hugh Miles, "The network covers Israeli affairs extensively, and is widely watched in Israel. In fact, Al Jazeera gives more air time to Israeli issues than any other channel outside Israel itself." All of this opens the network to the suspicion that they are pro-Israeli and pro-American; some in the Arab world even believe the station is funded by Mossad or the CIA.

Al Jazeera takes the controversy in stride and views this widespread criticism as the highest form of validation in journalism—if both sides are incensed by their coverage, they figure they must be doing something right. It's their own version of "fair and balanced."

Al Jazeera follows a strict, written code of ethics, which can be found on their website. For example, people often ask me if the network shows beheadings, and I can answer this question without hesitation or ambiguity: although Al Jazeera has broadcast tapes that include beheadings, they always stop the tape before the actual beheading. They have never shown a beheading, nor will they because it is against their code of ethics. The footage they have shown of the beheadings—for example those of Daniel Pearl in Pakistan and Nick Berg in Iraq—is identical to what U.S. news networks aired from the exact same tapes, though invariably some U.S.

media outlets will report in their headlines that Al Jazeera showed a beheading tape (without clarifying that it didn't show the tape's gruesome end).

Al Jazeera receives tapes from Al Qaeda in a variety of surreptitious ways: mailed to a bureau in Kabul, left on a doorstep in London, or delivered by a child in the streets of Cairo. They receive the tapes for the same reason the *New York Times* received the Unabomber's manifesto: the originators look for access to a large audience through a credible source. Wadah Khanfar, the director of Al Jazeera, points out that the network has received tapes from other insurgent groups (and at least six from Al Qaeda that the station has never aired), and that in terms of face time the network has shown far more of Bush and Blair than it ever has of Osama bin Laden.

But it's still an uphill battle. Jay Leno joked in his comedy routine, "we've killed Al Zarqawi. Of course, the question now is who will be the next Al Qaeda leader. Sounds like a bad reality show on Al Jazeera."

One of Al Jazeera's most popular shows is called *The Opposite Direction*, where host Faissal al Quasim invites people from polar opposite positions to engage in a debate. Anyone familiar with the shouting matches aired on western-world cable news would see this kind of show as a mixed-blessing, but the

Arab world had never witnessed such a spectacle—at least not on television. Before Al Jazeera, media in the Middle East used to be one-perspective, government-controlled television channels that preferred soap operas to news shows.

Faissal al Quasim's guests can say anything they want on *The Opposite Direction*, and he is probably the most trusted—and hated—man in the Middle East. *New York Times* columnist Thomas Friedman once protested while on the show that a cardboard cutout of him would serve its host's purposes just as well since the other guests spent most of their time screaming at him in Arabic. That day the program guests debated the concept of democracy, and a Jordanian intellectual had just claimed that the United States was the world's biggest dictatorship. Friedman ultimately admitted that Al Jazeera is "not only the biggest media phenomenon to hit the Arab world since the advent of television, it is also the biggest political phenomenon."

Friedman experienced firsthand Al Jazeera's influence throughout the Middle East. He left Qatar after the episode aired in November 2002 and went to Bahrain where, in a hotel lobby, a man went up to him and said, "Mr. Friedman, I saw you on Al Jazeera and I want you to know that that man you're on with was speaking nonsense; without democracy we'll never be able to grow." Later that same day, Friedman was approached by another man who said, "Mr. Friedman, I'm from Kuwait. I saw you on Al Jazeera. Without democracy we're lost." Then again, when Friedman left Bahrain, on the plane to London, the reserve pilot told him, "I just want you to know I watched that Al Jazeera show twice. I want you to know, without educational reform, we're never going to be able to develop."

Of all the show's guests, none has incited more controversy than Wafa Sultan. Sultan, a Syrian-born psychiatrist living in Los Angeles, appeared on *The Opposite Direction* on February 21, 2006, and argued with a prominent Muslim cleric. She criticized the corruption of the teachings of the Koran and decried the cultures of violence and barbarity that have been created in its name. She said things that no Arab woman had said before on an Arab network.

"The clash we are witnessing around the world is not a clash of religions, or a clash of civilizations," she said. "It is a clash between two opposites, between two eras. It is a clash between a mentality that belongs to the Middle Ages, and another mentality that belongs to the twenty-first century. It is a clash between civilization and backwardness, between the civilized and the primitive, between barbarity and rationality."

Her opponent, Dr. Ibrahim Al Khouli, tried to silence her as a heretic but he could not still her tongue. "The Jews have come from the tragedy [of the Holocaust] and forced the world to respect them with their knowledge, not with their terror; with their work, not their crying and yelling. . . . Only the Muslims defend their beliefs by burning down churches, killing people, and destroying embassies. This path will not yield any results. The Muslims must ask themselves what they can do for humankind, before they demand that humankind respect them."

That broadcast caused an uproar in both the Arab world and here in the West. Dr. Sultan received death threats as well as a book offer, while the video clip was e-mailed millions of times and became the talk of the blogosphere. Even my parents were e-mailed a link to the video and they forwarded it to me from Texas. When video snippets of a religious debate in Arabic are received in my parents' small town in Texas, you know the issue has achieved critical mass in our zeitgeist. Her dissent sparked an amazing debate that was followed throughout the whole world.

Progressive Arabs across the region may certainly like seeing religious bigotry challenged on television but derive even more pleasure and pride that Al Jazeera unflinchingly challenges the actions and ideals of Western powers. Westerners interviewed on Al Jazeera's programs are often caught off guard when they are not thrown the kind of softballs they have come to expect from their own national press. It also makes for good television when a government spokesperson drifts from the official speaking points. That happened, for example, to senior State Department official Alberto Fernandez, when he said in an interview broadcast on Al Jazeera in October 2006 that "there has been arrogance and stupidity" in the actions of the United States in Iraq. Though Fernandez was merely stating what is painfully obvious to most, and he is one of the few senior officials in the State Department who is fluent in Arabic, he later apologized and insisted that he misspoke.

It's almost impossible to overestimate the impact Al Jazeera has had on the Arab world, and it's difficult for a lot of westerners to comprehend how it is possible for this network to have gained such great influence in such a short time. The satellite network didn't so much reinvent journalism in the Middle East as invent it, or at least introduce it. Al Jazeera changed the way Arabs thought about the news in the same way Henry Ford changed the way Americans thought about travel.

While journalism in the United States has been around as long as the country itself—the radical pamphleteering of the Englishman Tom Paine led directly to his eyewitness accounts of the American Revolution, making him one of the world's first advocacy journalists as he wanted to see what his thinking had helped bring about—journalism arrived in the Middle East with other forms of western communication in the nineteenth century and was received with the sort of curiosity that greeted the first camel in the United States. The notion of a free press was anomalous. "The first newspapers were mainly official," Bernard Lewis wrote in *The Shaping of the Modern Middle East*. He continues:

> For example, the leading article in the first issue of the Ottoman official gazette, published on 14 May, 1832, defines the function of the press as being to make known the true nature of events and the real purpose of the acts and commands of the government, in order to prevent misunderstanding and forestall uninformed criticism, another purpose was to provide useful knowledge on commerce, science and the arts. The first nonofficial newspaper in Turkish was a weekly founded by an Englishman named William Churchill. It was followed by

many others, in Turkish, Arabic, and Persian, as well as other languages.[1]

With the division of the Middle East that followed the two world wars, the new Arab governments came to appreciate the power of the press. Even the less oppressive governments that didn't always suppress dissent made sure it didn't surface too often. "Journalists who have prepared articles which do not conform with the thinking of the regime have found that their material has not got into print, and they have been asked not to write any more—even though they have not necessarily been sacked," wrote Gerald Butt in his book *The Arabs: Myth and Reality*. He adds:

> This was the experience of the Egyptian writer Muhammed Sid Ahmed. During the Sadat presidency, he worked for the semi-official daily *Al-Ahram* and was critical of the President's policies. "I was pushed out of *Al-Ahram* for years," he said. "By 'out' I mean I was still on the payroll but nothing of mine was published. As the game is played, you see, there are ways by which you come to understand whether or not you are in their good books."[2]

Over time, independent newspapers that dared to challenge the various Arab states' governments were established. Although many of the newspapers cannot be published locally

---

1. Bernard Lewis, *The Shaping of the Modern Middle East* (Oxford University Press, 1994), p. 39.
2. Gerald Butt, *The Arabs: Myth and Reality* (I. B. Tauris, 1997), p. 166.

(such as the Saudi papers *Al Hayat* and *Asharq Al Awsat*, which are still published in London), they are widely read, largely by the intellectual class, throughout the Middle East. Still, finding alternative views to the government-approved ones isn't easy in the Middle East. "If you're an Egyptian or a Jordanian in the 1980s or early '90s your options are the local national TV station, which is incredibly boring, poorly produced and completely controlled by the ministry of information, and then national newspapers controlled by the government," says Marc Lynch, an associate professor of political science at Williams College and host of the popular Arab media blog site, Abu Aardvark. He adds, "Also, newspapers in the mid-90s, before Al Jazeera, were very expensive and didn't have wide circulation, so elite businessmen in luxury hotels read them, but the average person in most Arab countries just watched national TV and read national papers."

Though literacy is not the issue it once was, except in some remote rural areas, Al Jazeera's broadcastings gave large segments of the region's population access to independent news, bypassing the local governmental control of the most available media—a common reality until the '90s. Though it is hard to generalize about twenty-two different Arab countries, "You can safely say that Arab media before Al Jazeera was generally controlled, funded and censored by ministries of information," says Adel Iskandar, a scholar of Middle Eastern media and co-author of *Al Jazeera: The Story of the Network That Is Rattling Governments and Redefining Modern Journalism*. He explained in an interview,

These are not just regulatory institutions. These are incredibly powerful boards that determine everything about the news organization, from who gets hired and who gets fired all the way down to the miniscule details. There is commonly a review board that looks over every document published in the country before it actually goes to print. There was complete control of the media in virtually every Arab country. That's not to say there wasn't any independent journalism in countries like Lebanon and Egypt, but for the most part none of this was televised. The electronic media was always the terrain the governments needed to control completely and entirely.

That control ebbed away with the advent of satellite television. Suddenly governments could not dictate what was seen on television screens and the effects were jarring and somewhat humbling for audiences and journalists alike. "Satellite TV changed the Arab world on many levels," says Lawrence Pintak, who was the Middle East correspondent for CBS News in the 1980s. "People were hearing things they'd never heard before and seeing things they'd never seen before. But in addition, guys who were my contemporaries were almost embarrassed by their profession because they were so heavily controlled, and they were such mouthpieces for the government."

While many historians see the misinformation of the 1967 war as the turning point in Arab media, Pintak, who today directs the Adham Center for Electronic Journalism at the American University in Cairo, says the real "wake-up call came with the 1990–91 Gulf War, when all Arab eyes turned to CNN and BBC—or at least the eyes that belonged to people who spoke English. The official Saudi media did not mention the invasion of Kuwait for 36 hours. If you were a rich educated Saudi, who spoke English, you knew Iraqis had just invaded Kuwait, and you wanted to know about it, because you were next on the list."

Adel Iskandar experienced that invasion differently. He recalled,

> I was in Kuwait for the first Gulf War. I was subjected to the most horrendous Iraqi propaganda, to the point where we did not even realize that we had been invaded ten days into it. We thought there was a coup in Kuwait, somehow. That's the level of propaganda I'm talking about: where information is fabricated to such an extent that you are living in an illusion, that there is a whole mythology around you. What Al Jazeera did was question that mythology. After 1967, when Arab media lost its credibility, where did Arab audiences go? Literally for 30 years Arabs had to go to international news stations to get anything credible.

The Voice of America (VOA) was another reliable source, perhaps less so than the Paris-based Radio Monte Carlo, but still a reality check in the matrix of Arab propaganda.

According to Iskandar, VOA has lost its credibility in the Arab world as U.S. foreign policy has shifted right, "but then western broadcasters in Arabic were the only way we could find out what was happening around us. You would witness something in your backyard and have no idea what it was.

You had to listen to a station that broadcast from Cyprus to get news about your backyard."

Al Jazeera was born into this void. "The Emir of Qatar was perceptive in seeing the need to tap into that hunger," continues Iskandar, "to communicate with these people. When he did, that's when we had the Al Jazeera phenomenon. It's a perfect scenario in which you had a potential audience and a formula for success but nobody had the *cojones* to deliver. Anyone could have done it: Egypt could have done it, Iran could have done it. And at first it was perceived as something miniscule; no one believed it would go as far as it did."

At first, Al Jazeera was just a rumor in much of the Arab world. Before the station was widely included in various satellite broadcasting packages, VHS tapes of its debate shows could be bought on the black market in Damascus and Baghdad, areas where the network had no distribution. No one could quite believe what they were seeing. Iskandar says:

> I remember in the late '90s, you would flip through the channels on the satellite and as soon as you got to Al Jazeera, you knew you had entered a parallel world. And it wasn't just the level of debate; it was the kinds of things being talked about. You would never have seen a televised discussion on any Arab station about homosexuality; the notion was unheard of. Watching those kinds of shows was both horrifying for many traditionalists but incredibly refreshing for anybody who was used to the mundane, bland, tasteless coverage they've had for the last 30 or 40 years.
>
> They were the first Arab network to invite Israeli officials to come on. I cannot tell you how horrifying that

would be for an Arab audience in the late '90s: to turn on the television and see an Israeli speaking. Israelis had never spoken! One, they don't exist. Secondly, they don't speak. They just kill. For them to be involved in a dialogue was really just mind-boggling to an Arab audience.

Suspicions about the network sprang up like mushrooms—in whose interests was it to criticize Arab society and Arab governments? The answer was invariably the United States and Israel. Skeptics quickly pointed out that while the network broadcast lots of criticism about other countries, not much ill was said about the rulers of Qatar.

"Who cares?" replies Lynch, who is also the author of *Voices of the New Arab Public: Iraq, Al Jazeera and Middle East Politics Today.* Noting the nation's miniscule population he says:

> I have more people in my living room. It's a legitimate criticism but not all that compelling. Al Jazeera was pretty fiercely criticizing everyone else, which is why everyone got so upset with them. And the simple fact of criticism isn't new; you could always see criticism of Jordan by watching Syrian TV, for example. But the idea that they were adopting a critical perspective across the board was something new—especially when they were being critical of Saudi Arabia.

The adversarial relationship between Qatar and Saudi Arabia must be taken into account. As Pintak says, "The Emir didn't set up Al Jazeera to get a membership card at the press club. It's about power. This has allowed him to, if not checkmate, then at least occasionally check the Saudis. He did it for the same reason he brought Central Command to Qatar. It made him a player in the region and now Al Jazeera English makes him a player on the world stage."

Given its unique status in the Arab world, some critics contend that it's impossible to view Al Jazeera merely as a television network. "In many ways they set the agenda in the Arab world," says Iskandar, who also teaches international communications at American University in Washington, D.C. He adds:

> They have been consistently a de facto alternative voice in the Arab world for any respective regime or government. In many countries where there is no official opposition party, Al Jazeera became the opposition party. Which is quite peculiar: You never think of news organizations being political entities, and Al Jazeera isn't really a political entity. But because of their news style and formula—which is basically to challenge, whether it be [to] challenge power or challenge an audience member by presenting multiple sides of a story—what they inadvertently end up doing is representing the voices of those who have traditionally been silent.

Given the fate of many opposition parties in the Middle East, it is not surprising that the network dismisses such talk as hyperbole. In an interview with Pintak on the occasion of Al Jazeera's tenth anniversary in 2006, published on the progressive news site CommonDreams.org, Al Jazeera director

general Wadah Khanfar took pains to say, "We are not a political party; we are not a reform movement; we are a TV
station."

"The reality is, given the state of politics in the Arab
world, they are more than just a news organization," said
Pintak afterward. "They are a news organization that is creating change."

Change can be a mixed blessing, and having let the journalism genie out of the bottle, Al Jazeera may not like all of the
consequences. Lynch says:

> I've been making the argument for a while now. From
> 1997 to 2003, Al Jazeera had a monopoly; they were the
> only game in town and everybody watched it. They're still
> the number one station in the Arab world, and depending
> on the market they are a monopoly to strong competitors
> everywhere. But the Arab media TV market has gotten so
> competitive and so crowded that [Al Jazeera] faces stiff
> competition. Al Arabiya is the leading challenger, but in al-
> most every market there is at least one serious contender.

These competitors flatter the network sincerely, by imitat-
ing almost every aspect of Al Jazeera programming, from the
highly professional news coverage to the myriad talk shows.
"On the one hand you can say that this is the great achieve-
ment of Al Jazeera," continues Lynch. "It totally transformed

the TV market and everyone imitates them. The other side is that they can't single-handedly set the agenda anymore the way they once did. The exception is during times of crisis, like the Lebanon war, when they shoot to the top."

Most international critics praised the network's coverage of the 2006 conflict in Lebanon, as Al Jazeera once again filled the void in the Arab world. "In the first week to ten days of the Lebanon war, the official Saudi foreign policy was basically to blame Hezbollah and provide Israel with cover," says Lynch, adding:

> That meant that they underplayed the story. At the same time, Al Jazeera was flooding the zone and throwing everything they had at covering the story. On the one hand, people are angry; they're pissed at Israel and pissed at the U.S. and they know Al Jazeera is the place to go when they're feeling like that. So you have a combination of Al Jazeera covering it really well, people turning to Al Jazeera in times of crisis, and Al Arabiya, for political reasons, choosing to take itself out of the game. After ten days Al Arabiya's coverage changed, exactly when Saudi foreign policy changes—and people noticed that as well.

The independent Lebanese television stations were covering the conflict as well, but Al Jazeera was putting it in the context of a wider Arab narrative—something that was not lost on its Arab audience or its critics in the West. Indeed, the rap on Al Jazeera by many Western journalists has always been that they lack objectivity, identifying themselves as Arabs before they identify themselves as reporters.

There is a wonderful scene in *Control Room* in which Schleifer, who at the time had not yet joined Al Arabiya and had the job Lawrence Pintak now holds at the American University in Cairo, is lecturing a young reporter from Abu Dhabi TV about how to approach me in my capacity as a military spokesman. "Go talk to him, interview him, that's why he's here," advises Schleifer. "But smile when you talk to him." I think he just meant to tell him to be polite but you can see the young man bristle. He replies, "How can I smile when my people are being killed?"

"That really sums up the conundrum of Arab journalism," says Pintak, continuing,

> How can you be purely objective, if there is such a thing, in the western sense, if your people are being killed? The American media certainly wasn't after 9/11 because their people had been killed. . . . Then you put it in the context of a region that is in the throes of political changes of some sort—who the hell knows what it will ultimately be? But it's undergoing political and social change. So, is the role of Arab journalism to observe events, to drive events, to prevent events from taking place? Should the media be trying to overthrow governments? Should the media be supporting the Arab cause in issues like Iraq and Palestine? How you define the role of media is very much shaped by the situation on the ground at that time and place. Look at the American media at the time of the Revolution. It was anything but free, fair and balanced.

Iskandar thinks the objectivity argument is a bit of a canard and argues that Al Jazeera attempts to be objective by presenting multiple points of view—an approach to journalism that demands more of the audience. "Objectivity is being called into question not just by Al Jazeera but by all news organizations," he says, pointing to the "Fox News effect" within the United States as news networks sought to copy the network's success by being more opinionated in their reporting. "When 9/11 happened journalists went crazy in Manhattan—but it was not just about them being Americans, or that those individuals in the Twin Towers were Americans. It's about them being human. I think what we're asking journalists to do, especially when they are covering war, is not to be human."

Iskandar has no patience with the idea that Arabs can't quite grapple with objectivity and thinks that critics of Al Jazeera are missing the contributions the network has made to journalism as a whole. He says:

> Bernard Lewis and other neo-Orientalists have failed to recognize that Al Jazeera has taken a western approach to news and adapted it—and is now exporting it to the west. That idea is really quite mind-boggling. Arabs are supposed to be regressive, poor on information. They don't do anything right, they're irrational, they can't possibly deliver objective news. They're all about opinion; everything is contextualized. There is this idea that the Arab world is irrational and cannot be understood and doesn't behave properly. You're accustomed to this idea that the Arab world cannot produce anything good. What has the Arab world contributed to the world?

With his co-author Mohammed El Nawawy, Iskandar has coined the phrase "contextual objectivity" to describe what he considers the network's methodology—an approach he thinks will grow internationally. He states, "You can see the idea in Al Jazeera English that journalists are human beings and they are going to reverse the angle on the news by giving the voice to the people. It might sound clichéd but if they could do it in the Arab world, then they could do it elsewhere. They spent more time covering populist movements in the Arab world than they did covering heads of state, and that is not a coincidence but an orchestrated editorial decision on their part." He makes the point that the fifty-four countries of Africa, for instance, are all but invisible to American and even European audiences and states, "I think what Al Jazeera intends to do is take those individuals that are silent, absent or invisible in the international public agenda, and raise their stock, put them in a position where they are human beings."

Al Jazeera has brought about a definite sea change in the Arab world, one that veterans like Lawrence Pintak have been able to observe taking place over the last ten years. The same journalists who were once embarrassed to be working as mouthpieces for the government, are now feeling the yoke lift. He says, "Today those same guys are top editors, some of them on government-controlled newspapers, but even on government-controlled newspapers they see light at the end of the tunnel. They really see the potential for change and they are overtly pushing the envelope."

For Pintak, teaching journalism in Cairo, it is also a question of how this new tradition can build on the legacy of the west. He says:

I'm a child of the Watergate generation. I went to J school in '73 and we all wanted to be Woodward and Bernstein and change the world. I get that same sense from my students and young Arab journalists, whether they are in the Al Jazeera newsroom or working for *Al Ahram*, the Egyptian government newspaper. They see the possibility of changing things and they see the role that their profession can play in doing that. That is a direct response to the presence of Al Jazeera.

One of the things I try and teach my students is that they have to decide what shape Arab journalism will take. All we can and should do is expose them to mores and ideals, situations and lessons learned by American journalism and journalism elsewhere in the world, and let them decide what elements of that to bring to the table. It's not for me to tell an Arab journalist he shouldn't be showing graphic images of dead babies in Iraq when that is as much the truth as Marines being shot at.

For Iskandar, the U.S. audience needs to open its eyes. According to him, Americans stand to benefit the most from the sort of contextual objectivity a truly international journalism offers. From his home in Washington, D.C., he says:

All international news here seems to revolve around the possibility of the U.S. being threatened. And that's not the way news should be covered. I think Al Jazeera English is going to change the agenda, and that's been their slogan.

What has happened in countries where there is a growing and private independent media, is that Al Jazeera has raised the bar to such an extent that reporters and editors are pushing the envelope. I think they have created a sense of acceptability: it's acceptable to present alternative views, to challenge authority, to cover taboo topics.

Iskandar points to the story of the mob attacks on women that occurred in Cairo in November 2006: during Eid ul Fitr, the celebration that marks the end of Ramadan, hordes of young people filled Talat Harb Street in the center of the city in a scene like that of Times Square on New Year's Eve—but without police control. Whether the sexual abstinence that marks Ramadan was a factor or the crowd simply got out of hand, women were molested by gangs of young men. Some had their veils torn off. "They groped us in a way that was worse than anyone on the crowded street could imagine," a girl later told a reporter from *Al Ahram*. At first only silence marked the occasion, followed by denial, and almost no press coverage. Vicious rumors, authorities asserted, wild speculation, stories spread by enemies of the Arab people.

"Ultimately it called into question what it all means and what is happening in Egyptian society," says the Egyptian–Canadian Iskandar. "Have we lost our sensibility? Have we lost our humanity?" The story broke on a program called *Al Quahira Al Youm* on Dream TV, an independent network in Egypt. Using video and digital photos taken from revelers on the scene and relying on their eyewitness accounts, the program brought the story to national attention. He adds, "They would have never showed this before Al Jazeera came about. Before you knew it, this was the top story on other networks and then throughout the region, all thanks to Al Jazeera."

I had experienced Al Jazeera's methods firsthand when I was assigned to be Al Jazeera's liaison at CentCom. They didn't give me any special treatment—on the contrary. During one memorable incident on the air, one of Al Jazeera's producers set up an outside shot with me facing into a sand storm for an interview. The engineer ran for protection near the building, leaving me alone with the camera. A woman with a sweet, lilting British accent translated the host's Arabic words in my ear. I was being interviewed by someone I couldn't see, who was sitting in a comfortably air-conditioned studio not too far from CentCom. He was clearly hostile to the U.S. mission in Iraq, and I had only this disembodied voice to parry with. She asked everything very nicely with very little emotion.

"Is the U.S. military surprised by the fierce resistance of the Iraqi people to your invasion?" she asked sweetly.

"We are proceeding as planned, on our timetable," I replied. "We have encountered Fedayeen fighters who are not wearing military uniforms, which is a violation of the Geneva Conventions. But they have not impeded our progress."

"You say Saddam is violating the Geneva Conventions," she went on, "but the UN wrote the Geneva Conventions and the UN is against this war, so why should Saddam abide them?"

Still squinting into the sand, but at ease with her kind voice in my ear, I found myself nodding as I listened, when suddenly I realized: the host back in the studio is probably yelling at me, and the viewers, who only hear his voice and mine, must think I'm crazy or one sadistic son of a bitch. I'm just smiling at them and squinting and nodding despite the combative questions being bellowed at me.

With circumstances conspiring against me, my mind raced to piece an answer together. In a split second I reasoned: the third Geneva Convention, with the rules for the treatment of prisoners of war, was adopted in 1929; the UN was founded in 1945. I filled my lungs and let loose, "I'm afraid your question is built on a couple of false premises. The Geneva Conventions you're referring to predate the UN by 20 years, and the UN never passed a resolution for or against U.S. action in Iraq, but what's important about the Geneva Conventions is they're intended to reduce suffering for those who aren't fighting anymore, and for civilians who are caught in harm's way—that's our concern, the people of Iraq, and we wish they were Saddam's concern as well, but in every possible instance he's displayed that's not the case." I gasped for breath and waited for the next question.

At that point an Air Force lieutenant colonel came running out and joined me in the storm. "This is over!" he huffed, drawing his index finger across his throat. "You're done!" As we walked away he explained, "They hosed you. We were watching inside. They split the screen and were showing the bodies of women and children being pulled out of the rubble of some bombed Baghdad market alongside your face. It looked like you were talking about the bombing, as if we did it.

"That's it," he concluded. "No more interviews with Al Jazeera. You can't trust these people."

But I remember thinking that without our interviews, the bombed-out markets of the world would get the whole screen.

Seemingly immune to such criticism, Al Jazeera showed the human side of the invasion. The network was less interested in where the cruise missiles launched from than where they landed. For a force that rarely spoke of "collateral damage," the constant flow of images, from shredded bodies in the street to the bloodied, crying children in emergency rooms, was difficult to take. Rumsfeld accused Al Jazeera of faking these, which would be laughable if the pictures weren't so sad.

Al Jazeera Arabic also airs lighter fare. One of my favorite reporters for Al Jazeera Arabic is Nasser Hussaini, an espresso-loaded, cigarette-smoking, wry skeptic of a reporter. When I took my son Luke, 13 years old at the time, to the studios one day, we found Nasser finishing a surprisingly illuminating piece about America and the blues for which he had interviewed legendary guitarist Buddy Guy in Chicago. As he showed his clips to Luke in the edit bay, Nasser eagerly shared his newly found insight into the blues' origins, and hence rock music's origins, which he had grown up on. There was a voice-over in Arabic that Nasser translated for Luke as they watched.

"So the whole Arab world is going to watch a program about how the blues came from the old south to south Chicago?" Luke marveled.

"Yeah!" Nasser said. "When I was growing up in Morocco we were listening to Led Zeppelin and we had no idea that so much of their music came from the Mississippi Delta! We'd sing along with the lyrics with no idea what any of them meant. So this is not just about something American; this is about the roots of a music that we love, too."

I don't think a lot of people realize that Al Jazeera does stories on the blues—or modern-day American cowboys, or life on Indian reservations. Often Al Jazeera broadcasts some of the best aspects of the American experience to households throughout the Middle East, and Al Jazeera English will as well—dreams, warts, and all.

※

The peninsula of Qatar juts out from Saudi Arabia like a thumb from a hand—and the ruling tribes of Qatar and Saudi Arabia are ancient, mortal enemies. Mindful of Saudi Arabia's size (it has a landmass about 200 times larger and a population more than 20 times greater), and of the two nations' history of enmity, in 1996 the government of Qatar sought a bigger friend, and nothing secures steadfast allies faster than a 15,000-foot airstrip.

In the same year it founded Al Jazeera, Qatar also built the largest airfield in the Middle East, Al Udeid Air Base, and offered it to the United States to use indefinitely, if U.S. forces were so inclined. Today, the air base, which, despite its size, was something of a secret before the U.S.-led invasion of Afghanistan in 2002, can accommodate up to 10,000 U.S. troops and 120 aircraft. Confident, with the United States as an ally, the government of Qatar sold most of its air force to India. The threat of a Saudi invasion no longer worries them—though the Saudis certainly regard Al Jazeera as something of an intrusion.

The Saudis harbor intense jealousy of the relationship Qatar has with the U.S. government, and it's rumored that they are behind AlJazeera.com—a website purportedly pertaining to a Dubai magazine founded in 1992, which maintains a Dubai address but has London phone numbers. This is not the official website of Al Jazeera, but the first one many people find when looking for the network's URL, and some believe the Saudis operate it in an effort to smear the network's reputation. If so, the site enjoys great success, as it is undoubtedly the world's leading source of misinformation about Al Jazeera television network.

I visited that website by mistake when Al Jazeera first contacted me about working for them and a friend of mine suggested I check out their website. On that day, early in 2005, AlJazeera.com's lead story explained how the United States caused the tsunami by testing nukes in the Pacific. Another piece told how Rumsfeld was busy planning a second set of 9/11 attacks because the first set had gone so well for him. You could also read an opinion column on when it was okay to beat one's wife, according to the Koran. A quick call to Al Jazeera cleared up the issue for me; the official website is www.aljazeera.net/english.

Al Jazeera sued over the name at the World Intellectual Property Organization in Geneva, Switzerland, back in 2005, but lost because the dot-com domain had been registered first and because of the commonness of the name: *al jazeera*, which means "the peninsula" in Arabic, is a popular business name, given to restaurants, taxicabs, and barbershops throughout the Arab world.

Although a failed URL dispute may seem like a small thing, in a time when airwaves have superseded oceans in connecting the world, such a defeat may be compared to the Royal Navy's defeat in the second Anglo-Dutch War. It was a strategic setback. Just as England's huge navy spanned the globe during the colonial days and solidified the nation's status as a world power for three centuries, Qatar's position is much the same today in the realm of information. The small nation has expanded its reach globally through its energy resources, education, and, most importantly, satellite television. Having begun by emulating Western media, Al Jazeera hopes to surpass them; by going international the network plans to actively compete with both BBC World and CNN International.

CHAPTER SIX
THE GROUND TRUTH ABOUT AL JAZEERA

Americans have a morbid interest in Al Jazeera. The network has been so demonized by both the U.S. media and government that first-time watchers might expect horns and tails on the anchors, or, at the very least, some sort of "Terrorist TV," as it has been branded. If Bush is joking about bombing the network's headquarters, located in Doha, the capital of an allied nation, the stuff they're broadcasting must be pretty bad.

Whenever American networks rebroadcast bin Laden tapes they make no effort to hide Al Jazeera's famous logo on the footage and they lead the story with the news that Al Jazeera showed another Al Qaeda tape today. It's become the American networks' makeshift disclaimer for showing bin Laden dispatches. The truth is that Al Jazeera has sharing agreements (meaning they share footage) with CNN, ABC, NBC, and Fox News—agreements that were sought out by U.S. networks in an effort to show the exclusive videos and satisfy viewer demand.

Al Jazeera is broadcast by satellite in the United States and lays claim to quite a broad viewership in any area with a large Arab-American population. As important as it may seem, non-Arab speakers have but a pale idea of the network's enormous influence in the Middle East. To get a sense of Al Jazeera's importance in the Arab world you have to see it in context, firsthand, in the region.

An Army colonel who had spent some time in the Middle East told me he had been in Kuwait, at the home of that nation's defense minister, when the U.S. Congress was conducting its hearings into the Abu Ghraib scandal. "The Kuwaiti official had this huge TV," he recalled, "and he was glued to the screen. It turned out Al Jazeera was showing the hearings in their entirety, as if they were C-SPAN, and this guy couldn't believe what he was seeing."

"I don't understand," the defense minister asked the colonel. "Why are these government officials asking questions of other government officials? Don't they all work for the same government?"

"Yes," the colonel explained, "but these elected officials are trying to hold these military officials accountable. Otherwise it looks like the entire government is condoning what happened at Abu Ghraib."

The Kuwaiti defense minister couldn't quite wrap his mind around the paradigm: a government holding itself accountable. If a silver lining to the Abu Ghraib scandal can be found, perhaps it's that in addition to Al Jazeera showing the pictures of abused prisoners, this time rebroadcast from a U.S. media exclusive, the network also showed the ensuing investigative hearings—and covered them a lot more thoroughly than American news networks did. Viewers in the Arab world took away a civics lesson: that, whatever its faults, the U.S. system struggles to keep itself in check. Without trying to shape the story, but by showing it all, Al Jazeera allowed its viewers a more complex picture of the Abu Ghraib story and, ultimately, of the United States.

If the defense minister took pause at the hearings, imagine the reaction of the ordinary citizens who were watching: "*That's* what a government is supposed to do?"

The outrage over Al Jazeera in the United States often seems to boil down to the fact that they allow airtime to perspectives that are not deemed politically correct according to mainstream American standards. For instance, many Americans aren't used to seeing anyone try to put Al Qaeda in any context other than "evil," and they aren't accustomed to being presented a perspective from someone they consider a terrorist.

The word "terrorism" seems to have lost its meaning in the United States. Terrorism means taking violent action against targets that aren't militarily or politically justifiable for the purpose of inducing fear. More and more often, instead, I find that the word terrorism is used—here in the United States—to label anything that is directed against America. This is how critics get away with labeling Al Jazeera "Terrorist TV."

Indeed, Al Jazeera will openly broadcast anti-American sentiment on the network, just as it will strive to find a counterbalance to such positions in an effort to allow its audience both perspectives. The United States receives no special treatment—governments across the Middle East and throughout the world experience similar criticism and analysis on the network. Al Jazeera is committed to allowing voices such as Wafa Sultan's to be heard. "The opinion and the other opinion" is the motto of Al Jazeera, and while that may sound better in Arabic, the meaning is the same in any language.

The myth that Al Jazeera is a tool for the terrorists thrives to this day, probably because the network remains the best method for reaching a widespread Arab audience. In the spring of 2006, a bin Laden audio tape came out in which he commented on Zacarius Moussaoui's trial and on two Al Jazeera employees who have been arrested: Sami Al Hajj, a cameraman being held in Guantanamo, and Tayseer Allouni, a reporter under house arrest in Spain. In the tape, bin Laden denies that either of these men are connected with Al Qaeda. Al Jazeera, regularly hailed as the mouthpiece of Al Qaeda, aired the tape as part of the news program and then moved on to a soccer game. CNN continued to show the same bin Laden message, scrutinized by analysts, on a continuous loop for the rest of the day, yet no one honestly believes that CNN is the mouthpiece of bin Laden.

In September 2006, Al Jazeera broadcast another tape it had received from Al Qaeda, which showed bin Laden purportedly planning the 9/11 attacks. The reel contained a sophisticated piece of propaganda by Al Qaeda standards. Martyr videos of hijackers Hamza Al Ghamdi and Wail Al Shehri were included with images of the Twin Towers of the World Trade Center burning behind them as they spoke: planning and execution, past and future, in one jihad instant. American networks showed only short sections from the video.

Al Jazeera came under attack as usual, but the network's critics failed to acknowledge the powerful backlash against bin Laden that showing the entire tape created among the Arab audience. A good deal of the Arab world still believes the Saudi-born militant Islamist had little or nothing to do with 9/11 and claims the terrorist attacks resulted, instead, from a U.S.-Zionist conspiracy. (Sadly, an alarming number of Americans—more than a third, according to a 2006 Scripps Howard/Ohio University poll—believe something similar.[1]) For many throughout the Arab world, actually seeing bin Laden plan the 9/11 attacks finally confirmed his guilt; by airing bin Laden's tape in full, Al Jazeera played a crucial role in the process.

The U.S. government would be wise to recognize the value of Al Jazeera's reach in the Middle East, as its viewers regard the network as "the most trusted name in news." If the United States would accept using the network as an emissary, their messages to the Arab world would be tempered with a much greater credibility than could be gained through domestic networks. The government must relinquish control of the message, though, and allow Al Jazeera to give it the same coverage and diligence the network insists for other stories.

The first tapes implicating bin Laden in 9/11 were found by Marines searching a house in Kandahar. They were handed over to the U.S. State Department, who scrutinized them for clues regarding Al Qaeda or messages to terrorist cells, before copying and distributing them to the media. The footage played to the consternation of some in the United States and abroad, who continued to insist on bin Laden's innocence. Americans hold a double standard regarding the distribution of bin Laden's tapes—U.S. media is allowed full access, while Al Jazeera is branded the mouthpiece of Al Qaeda. Most people forget or don't know that our government was Al Qaeda's first tape distributor in the United States.

---

1. http://www.scrippsnews.com/node/10523

The U.S. government often denies Al Jazeera access to official spokespeople. In particular, the Arab network's reporters are not allowed in American-occupied Iraq, and their calls to U.S. officials often go unanswered, a myopic and counterproductive policy.

A telling scene in *Control Room* follows Al Jazeera producer Samir Khader as he interviews an American "political analyst" by the name of Jeffrey Steinberg. Samir asks some fairly open-ended questions about U.S. interests in Iraq, and then translates Steinberg's answers into Arabic: the United States wants to become an empire, control Iraq's oil reserves, and so on. Samir cuts the interview short and, overcome with frustration, reprimands the booker.

"Where did you get that guy!" he yells. "He's just a crazy activist!"

"But he was analyzing," the producer protests.

"That was not analysis—that was hallucination!" When he calms down he explains that Steinberg would be fine on a talk show, "but not on our news program. There we want guests who are balanced. We want guests who can give us both sides of the story."

By refusing to submit to interviews or engage in debate on the network, the U.S. government also deprives Al Jazeera's coverage and viewers of a balanced viewpoint, and instead allows the extreme positions of those on the left or the right to take over.

For instance, Debbie Schlussel writes a right-wing blog and is no stranger to the pundit world of talk radio and cable news. She credits herself with having exposed Caribou Coffee for its supposed terrorist ties, and after faking her way into a mosque in Dearborn, Michigan, Schlussel proclaimed that anti-American propaganda was being preached from the pulpit there. She also called me "the biggest boob in America" for going to work for Al Jazeera English. (She claims that her online popularity in the political realm is second only to that of Ann Coulter, so I guess I should be honored, though her summation of my career in the Marines and everything after contained so many errors of fact that I find it hard to imagine she gets much of anything else right.) Al Jazeera's reporters, she maintains, moonlight as terrorists and the network's hosts issue fatwas against infidels.

You can imagine my surprise, then, at seeing her name as an upcoming guest on an Al Jazeera Arabic program. I contacted Al Jazeera's booker and asked her if the network was paying Schlussel to appear. The program was in a bind and needed someone to fill the chair—our booker reasoned that Schlussel was only offered a few hundred dollars. Schlussel told her readers she would be going into "the belly of the beast." (With a little something for her troubles. . . .) The pundits affiliated with the right-wing think tanks are famous for going where the money is. I'm sure they would defend themselves by saying they are just trying to bring their perspective to a diverse audience, but the practice still makes for some strange bedfellows.

I witnessed the same phenomenon in my capacity as a host on Al Jazeera English. We were shooting a pilot of a talk show when I met another hardline female conservative, Danielle

Pletka of the American Enterprise Institute, a conservative think tank based in Washington, D.C. On set before the cameras rolled, I mentioned I was surprised, given her pedigree, to see her there.

"You're paying me," she said, huffily. "There is no way I would set foot here if you weren't."

Schlussel later wrote on her blog, "But this morning, I was on the belly of the beast, Al-Jazeera. That's right, the Terrorist News Network. I have made my negative feelings about the network clear and am frightened by its efforts to get a full-time English-language network in place."[2]

So both Schlussel and Pletka believe Al Jazeera is a terrorist organization that should be treated as an enemy of the United States; they would never lower their good names by appearing on such a dangerous network, unless of course they were paid $300.

Because official U.S. government spokespeople aren't *available* to get the message out to the folks who need the most convincing (as opposed to the amen choir at Fox News), Al Jazeera often must rely on partisan conservatives who only appear for money, or equally doctrinaire "left-wing activists" who show up anywhere to denounce Bush and promote Ralph Nader. I don't know which group is worse, the partisans or the progressives, though in a time of war I suspect the latter. When we most need someone to

---

2. http://www.debbieschlussel.com/archives/2006/02/me_on_al-jazeer.html.

explain military action, you don't want to send in the Peace Corps instead of the Marine Corps.

Engaging all sides needs to be standard operating procedure for our government on this new media battleground, otherwise they are simply ceding the turf to the other side. Steinberg doesn't represent Americans any better than Pletka does. State and Defense Department officials of the highest level should be appearing on Al Jazeera regularly, for the same reason Israel encourages its government representatives to do so: it's good for the cause. Even if the Arab audience might not like what the U.S. government has to say, it should see the benefit of arguing its case intelligently, thus possibly deflating some of America's demonization that otherwise might go unchecked.

⸱⸱⸱

The Arab world extends unmatched credibility to Al Jazeera. In a region where watching television is a communal activity, where images are broadcast 24/7 in coffee houses, barbershops, grocery stores, and pharmacies, a 24-hour news channel emerges as a powerful organization. In fact, a 2006 global survey by BrandChannel.com ranked Al Jazeera 19th on their list of brands with the most global impact. To put this into perspective, McDonald's, which boasts over 31,000 restaurants and employs more than 1.5 million people worldwide, placed 22nd. Considering BBC and CNN—the only other news media on the list—finished 27th and 43rd respectively, Al Jazeera can arguably be considered the most influential news brand across the world. The network hopes to expand that credibility and global outreach with the addition of Al Jazeera English as they open bureaus in places such as Zimbabwe, Iran, and Somalia, where most other international news agencies cannot, or will not, go.

I've heard pundits complain about the rock-star status of Hassan Nasrallah, the leader of Hezbollah. His first appearance in Beirut after the Israeli-Lebanese war drew hundreds of thousands of supporters. Hezbollah orchestrated the event with great attention to detail, and yes, it is legitimate to question the wisdom of people celebrating a nongovernmental organization that has just invited death and destruction into their country—as Hezbollah did when it captured Israeli soldiers. But the rally was not an entirely surprising phenomenon—the Lebanese didn't seem to have any hard feelings, or they certainly weren't on display, as Hezbollah helped rebuild places Israel had destroyed, loaning money to homeowners, even as the United States and the United Nations lent little but lip service. Al Jazeera had no choice but to give that rally, and its celebrity, the kind of coverage it did. To do otherwise would have made them look suspect to their Arab viewers, or at least something less than credible.

But the network doesn't need to feed the narrative, or to try to shape that story. A friend of mine from Lebanon who works at AAI, Rebecca Abou-Chedid, pays close attention to the news in the Arab world and how it reflects, or distorts, the interest of the diverse population there. "You have to remember that most of the Arab world is Sunni," she recently told me over coffee. "They don't want to empower a Shi'ite leader like Nasrallah, backed by Iran. They are giving him his due—but I don't think he's who a lot of them would have picked as a hero."

She gives credit to Al Jazeera for playing the story straight down the middle—just as they did in their coverage of the detainee interrogation (or torture) bill that Congress sent to Bush in September 2006. What got more press in the Middle East than here, she said, was the language in the bill that denied habeas corpus rights—the right to go to court to protest detention and treatment—to anyone the federal government accuses of terrorism.

> Arab-American citizens could be denied the right of habeas corpus—a right guaranteed in the U.S. Constitution—for "aiding and abetting the enemy," even if they had no idea they were doing so. An Arab-American in New York or Michigan or California could be jailed for giving money to a mosque, thinking it was for food or hospitals in the Middle East, when it's discovered that the money actually went to buy arms. And they could do nothing to protest their treatment, even though it is their inalienable right as American citizens to do so! The Bush administration denies this could happen, but their credibility is suspect. In the Arab world, this makes the United States look like a big fat hypocrite.

The "big fat hypocrite" line is one I often use in my public speeches when the questions turn to how the United States is perceived in the Arab world. To preach human rights, and then deny them to some people some of the time, all under the guise of a never-ending, know-it-when-we-see-it "war on terror," looks all too familiar to a lot of people in the Middle East. Look at the United States' relationship with Saudi Arabia's government (certainly not democratically elected, compared to Hamas, for example). Many Arab governments' modi operandi are to prosecute its citizens without having to justify the reasons, to make them disappear and then question the motives and loyalty of anyone who suspects their tactics.

In 2006, during the outbreak of widespread protests and riots in response to the publication in Denmark of cartoons that depicted the prophet Mohammed, two Jordanian editors were arrested for publishing the cartoons, alongside commentary, on whether the violent reaction to the cartoons was wrong and harmful to the perception of Islam to the rest of the world. One of the journalists, Jihad Momani, wrote in his commentary "what brings more prejudice against Islam, these caricatures or pictures of a hostage taker slashing the throat of his victim in front of the cameras, or a suicide bomber who blows himself up during a wedding ceremony in Amman?" He was arrested and charged with insulting religion and sentenced to two months in prison. In Yemen, three journalists were detained and three publications were closed for printing the cartoons.

Most Arab governments are totalitarian and do not tolerate a critical media. Israel is one of the few countries in the Middle East that has not banned Al Jazeera's reporters because it has historically valued the right to free speech and a free press. These concepts don't get a lot of play in countries like Kuwait, Bahrain, Saudi Arabia, or Oman. The government officials in those countries are still infuriated when members of any media question them, whether the reporter is one of their own or from a neighboring country.

But the power of the media transcends the old idea of kingdom rule; it crosses the lines that have been drawn in the sand. Those governments may not allow Al Jazeera's reporters into their countries, but their citizens' ubiquitous satellite dishes pick up the network's signal. Families and members of communities gather around television sets in homes, cafes, and bazaars to watch the news on Al Jazeera. The closest parallel in American history that comes to mind is Franklin Delano Roosevelt's fireside chats that were delivered over the radio—but Al Jazeera doesn't speak with one voice and doesn't have a political agenda.

Not that I expect the Bush administration to reach out to Al Jazeera anytime soon: in November 2005, the British newspaper *The Daily Mirror* reported on a leaked memorandum in which Blair and Bush talked about bombing Al Jazeera headquarters in Doha. While officials of both governments have been silent in response to questions about the incident, with some suggesting it was a joke, the British government is prosecuting the government official who took the conversation seriously enough to leak it to the press.

For many, the idea of America bombing a television network sounds absurd, but Al Jazeera employees have learned to take these claims seriously after their bureaus in Kabul and Baghdad were both bombed by the United States, killing one reporter and wounding several others. In the case of the Kabul office, the United States claimed that members of Al Qaeda had been spotted walking in and out the building—yet they bombed the building when no one was there. Ron Suskind, author of *The One Percent Doctrine*, said emphatically to Wolf Blitzer on CNN's *Situation Room:* "My sources are clear that that was done on purpose, precisely to send a message to Al Jazeera, and essentially a message was sent." As for the bombing of the Baghdad building, the official explanation maintains that U.S. forces didn't know the building contained an office of Al Jazeera. (I maintain the Baghdad bombing was not intentional; see my discussion of this in chapter three). Al Jazeera's Washington, D.C., studios are near 16th and K streets, three blocks from the White House; so, should our government decide to revisit the bombing idea, they would have to worry about collateral damage at the president's home, or so goes the joke around the studio.

My friend Abderrahim Foukara is now the chief of Al Jazeera Arabic's Washington, D.C., bureau, but previously he covered UN proceedings and he was working when the United

Nations released their report on the assassination of the former prime minister of Lebanon, Rafik Hariri, on October 20, 2005. The results of the investigation had been highly anticipated in the Arab world and, as everyone suspected, the report implicated the government of Syria. What happened that evening has become part of international broadcast lore. Foukara described the incident when he was a guest on *The Charlie Rose Show* (along with Warren Hoge of the *New York Times* and Raghida Dergham of the Beirut newspaper *Al Hayat*) the following evening.

"What happened on Al Jazeera?" Rose asked. "I wish I had a video of this."

"What happened was quite interesting, even surreal," said Foukara, who is one of the most urbane and eloquent people you could ever meet. If he says something was interesting or surreal, you know he isn't exaggerating. He told his host that he had called Doha to say that he had the report at a little before 7 PM, and the producers asked him if he could join them live at the top of the hour to discuss the gist of it.

Foukara continued, "So I go on the air with this report and the first question is, 'What's in it?' And I said, 'I only just got it, I cannot tell you with any certainty exactly what's in it.'"

Foukara then said that he began to read what looked to him like salient passages from the report when another voice from Doha, of someone that sounded to him as pro-Syrian, started to quibble with the piecemeal nature of his reporting.

"His argument was, 'You cannot just pick and choose,'" Foukara recalled, "he said it was way too early to discuss it."

At this point one of Foukara's bosses had spoken into his ear-piece: "We're going to try and have you read the report in full," he said.

"I thought it was a joke," Foukara told Rose and his guests. "It's fifty-four pages long." Then he heard an Al Jazeera announcer say, "And now we join our correspondent live in New York, who will read the UN's report in its entirety."

"So I sat there and read that report, all fifty-four pages, both sides, live on air, while somebody in Doha was doing simultaneous translation," concluded Foukara.

Foukara's fellow journalists on the show were very amused. Lebanese paper *Al Hayat*'s lead reporter Dergham had been asked by NBC to comment on the incident. "Let me find something interesting and translate it," he said.

But Al Jazeera, goaded perhaps by a skeptic in its studio, had reacted differently. "I started reading it at about 7:30," said Foukara to Rose, "and I finished at exactly ten minutes to midnight."

"How many viewers do you think you had with you at that point?" asked Hoge, who was probably trying to imagine an American news network giving its entire evening over to a similar reading.

"Probably two households," Foukara replied, "but probably every government in the region."

CHAPTER SEVEN
WHAT THEY DON'T KNOW CAN KILL US

The United State's current "no comment" approach to the Arab media is dangerous. Imagine the following scenario: Marines patrol past a mosque in a village and are fired upon from inside the mosque. The Marines return fire as per the rules of engagement with disproportionately effective and destructive force. A news team shows up at the end of the firefight. For the young Marines, the rules of engagement are equally clear about responding to a reporter—it's a "no-go." Despite the reporter's best efforts to get a statement from one of the Marines about the engagement, the journalists only hear "no comment" instead. After the squad departs the area, an Arab fighter approaches the reporter and gives an emotionally animated interview, "They are attacking the mosques! We were praying inside. Look at what they've done!" Never mind the bullet holes in the wall across the road from the mosque.

The reporter contacts the squad's base to no avail, especially if the journalist is Arab. The reporter then calls a public affairs office in Baghdad (one of many) and is referred to another public affairs office, where he or she will either be referred again or they may take the question and offer a call back. If the office discovers the reporter works as a stringer for Al Jazeera, the journalist will get no further. Eventually, the reporter is forced to run with the story as is—if he or she is a good reporter, he or she will mention that there seemed to be evidence refuting that one interviewee's claim, but the U.S. military declined to comment. "No comment" often implies culpability and a cover up in every culture. If the reporter is frustrated with the military's stonewalling, the refuting evidence may not even make it into the story.

Reporters, regardless of their nationalities or affiliates, run with what they have because deadlines must be met. When the footage airs across the Middle East, showing Marines firing on a mosque and an Arab eyewitness screaming that they were peacefully praying when blood-lusting

Marines mercilessly attacked, young Arabs watching the news on Al Jazeera might conclude they have the responsibility to fight the infidels who assault their mosques and the pious Muslims within. What begins as a tactical error quickly escalates into a regional strategic problem, propelled by the catalyst of "no comment."

This same story has played out time and again, for years now. And the people implementing the "no comment" policy are the same ones who complain that Al Jazeera is one-sided. Of course they'll be one-sided on stories involving the U.S. government, if the government won't give its side. Administration-appointed civilians at the Pentagon commonly forbid the military to speak to Al Jazeera, but the policymakers won't go on-air to defend their policies, either—thus leaving the network with the think-tank extremists of the right and the blogosphere idealists of the left. The resulting stories make Americans look like fools or cynics.

This ideologically pure, if ill-informed, no-access policy handed down from the White House and the Pentagon has real consequences: real people plant bombs in marketplaces or on roadsides; real people hijack planes, armed with little more than box cutters and a pure, if ill-informed, ideology of their own. For what must seem like a matter of principle to someone in Washington, D.C., the consequences play out in the Middle East in real life-and-death scenarios and eventually may very well be experienced on U.S. soil, again.

No one feels more frustrated by this than those members of the military who are closest to the consequences. I have received e-mails and phone calls from commanders in Iraq who have said, "We think you're right about Al Jazeera. The military needs to work with them." They want to engage the network through me but their hands have been tied.

In March 2006, I got an e-mail from a public affairs officer in Fallujah, Major Riccoh Player (Major Player is widely known to have one of the all-time, great rank-name combinations), saying he had attended a morning meeting where a Marine general requested to have me embedded. "He made it an order for us to get you here."

I called my friend Major Todd Breasseale, who was in charge of handling the media for one of the public affairs offices in Baghdad. "Looks like I'm going to come see you," I said. "They want me to embed in Fallujah." But then a public affairs officer, Lieutenant Colonel Barry Johnson (from a different office in the convoluted command structure over in Iraq), caught wind of the plan and vetoed the visit. A friend told me that not only was I not allowed to come into the country, but it was said that public affairs officers shouldn't even be communicating with me because I'm with Al Jazeera.

Although I would many months later receive the green light to visit Iraq as a journalist, my first attempt illustrates the deep divisions that exist within the military about Al Jazeera. I've yet to find a soldier with a mild opinion of Al

Jazeera. They either believe the network is part of the problem and should be obstructed or they believe it could be part of the solution and should be engaged as much as possible. There is no middle ground, at least not that I've found.

In September 2004, Al Jazeera was barred from Iraq by the Iraqi government. The network had been temporarily banned earlier that year because it broadcast accusations regarding Israel's interest in Iraq. The comments had not been made by an Al Jazeera reporter or host, but uttered by an *Iraqi* guest on the *Opposite Direction* program, and refuted by the show's other guest, another Iraqi official. Can you imagine the outrage that would ensue if NBC were booted from America for comments made by some radical guest on one of its talk shows? Indeed, many U.S. programs interview extremists—members of Ku Klux Klan, say, or the Black Panthers—just to engender controversy and give the host the opportunity to play the good guy and denounce prejudice.

Off the record, both military and Iraqi officials admitted that Al Jazeera's ban related more to their belief that the network was inciting violence in Iraq and the *Opposite Direction*'s segment merely provided Iraqi officials with a smokescreen.

Since Al Jazeera has left Iraq, though, the violence has escalated exponentially—at the time of this writing, an attack occurs on U.S. troops in Iraq every fifteen minutes. Iraqi and

U.S. officials alike refuse to acknowledge that the suppression of Al Jazeera's coverage from within Iraq has not diminished the violence—it has only escalated. The ban has, in effect, silenced Iraqi and U.S. voices from presenting their viewpoint to the most trusted news source not only in Iraq, but in the entire Arab-speaking world as well.

The military has made some efforts in trying to communicate with the Arab media, even if they seem to lack the full commitment of the brass. A friend of mine, an Army reservist who served with me at CentCom, knows the stakes in this media battle. In conjunction with his boss, a navy captain reservist, he recently opened a U.S. military office in Dubai with a mission to reach out to the Arab press.

It's great that the military has opened such an office, but to have two reservists—even if they are two of the best public affairs officers I know—trying to engage all the Arab media on behalf of the American military is an underwhelming effort.

It's difficult to know what sort of clearance this outreach program has from the officials within the puzzle palace that is the Pentagon. These two guys are supposed to regularly call Al Jazeera and Al Arabiya and say, "Is there anything I can help you with? Is there a story you need our resources for? Can I help you get access to anyone?"

I told my friend my mosque story and he said, "Part two happens after your reporter tries going through official channels to find the Marines' side of the story. He files his report, and after it is translated into English and brought to the attention of the senior leadership in Baghdad, a general will call my office and say, 'You need to get on top of this story, there is some serious misinformation here.' So I will call Al Jazeera and say, 'You missed our perspective'—72 hours later! But half a dozen similar stories have occurred since then and sometimes they don't even know which attack I'm referring to."

The news cycle always rolls on and my friend, despite his best efforts, is left out in the desert, spinning his wheels.

Shortly after invading Iraq, the United States attempted to circumvent Al Jazeera by establishing its own Arabic language satellite television network, Al Hurra ("The Free One"). Al Hurra is commercial free, and free to satellite dish subscribers whether they want it or not—but many in Iraq regard Al Hurra with skepticism and would not consider tuning in to the network for an independent (or "free") perspective. As noted on the front page of Al Hurra's website, alhurra.com, the network is "operated by a non-profit corporation, The Middle East Broadcasting Networks, Inc (MBN). MBN is financed by the American people through the US Congress."

Just like the war.

Al Hurra was launched in 2004 with great fanfare and an exclusive interview with Bush—and was immediately lambasted by critics in the Arab world and in the United States. "Al Hurra, like the U.S. government's Radio Sawa and *Hi* magazine before it, will be an entertaining, expensive and irrelevant hoax," said Al Jazeera's Rami Khouri, and added, "Why do they keep insulting us like this?" The *Washington Post* was even more unforgiving. "[Al Hurra] has a chance of turning out to be one of this country's most ill-conceived and wasteful experiments ever in public diplomacy," the paper said, before moving on to wonder who, exactly, the audience was supposed to be.[1]

Viewers stayed away, and small wonder. People in the Arab world are all too familiar with state-controlled media, press organs that run only good news about the king or government, and bad news about any dissidents or insurgents. Under Saddam, a media consortium of eighteen television stations, a number of radio stations, and a national newspaper existed. Uday, Saddam's notorious son, oversaw them all and all were filled with content the dictator had sanctioned. The CPA had replaced Saddam's stations with the Iraqi Media Network (IMN)—a sort of precursor of Al Hurra—and the network had proven a dismal failure as well, with the BBC reporting that most Iraqis thought the IMN was "a mouthpiece for the CPA."

Propaganda machines are prone to breaking down, no matter how pure the intentions. Before the United States invaded Iraq, Charlotte Beers was appointed "undersecretary of state for public diplomacy" and put in charge of the Shared Values campaign in the Middle East. A former adver-

---

1. Rami Khouri, quoted in Hugh Miles, *Al Jazeera: The Inside Story of the Arab News Channel That Is Challenging the West* (Grove Press, 2005), p. 375; *Washington Post*, April 4, 2003, p. A21.

tising executive at J. Walter Thompson and Ogilvy & Mather, Beers was tasked to convince the Arab world that Americans weren't so bad after all. Beers had the full blessing of her boss: Powell told NBC, "She got me to buy Uncle Ben's Rice. So there is nothing wrong with getting somebody who knows how to sell something."[2]

Uncle Sam proved a tougher sell than Uncle Ben.

Though the U.S. State Department defended Beers' campaign, "Those spots were only intended to run during the month of Ramadan, and they were completed success-fully on schedule,"[3] Beers resigned in March 2003 after two years of trying to get the U.S. point of view across to a hostile audience (one of her innovations involved dispatching a point man fluent in Arabic to speak on Al Jazeera every time a bin Laden tape aired), citing health reasons.

Three months later, and after the Pew Research Center for the People released dismal statistics on the United States's image in the Middle East, the U.S. State Department investigated the failure of the Shared Values mission.

In addition to the Shared Values campaign and the IMN, the U.S. government spent an additional $100 million on Al Hurra to prove once again that state-run propaganda doesn't change the hearts and minds of anyone.[4] During his disas-

---

2. Norman Solomon, *War Made Easy: How Presidents and Pundits Keep Spinning Us to Death* (John Wiley & Sons, 2005), p. 25.
3. Richard Boucher, spokesman, from a U.S. State Department press briefing, October 30, 2002, http://www.state.gov/p/nea/rls/rm/14835.htm.
4. Miles, *Al Jazeera*, p. 374.

trous war, Lyndon Johnson often referred to winning the "hearts and minds" of the Vietnamese. The phrase has since become a cliché in military IO, or information operations, shorthand for a failure of intelligence and imagination. Just say "hearts and minds" and people know the topic of discussion is dead in the water.

Just as Johnson and other architects of the Vietnam War believed they could, and should, win the hearts and minds of the Vietnamese people, I'm sure someone in the Bush administration believed a government-created press would be attractive to the Arab world. The same logic had guided Radio Marti, the "Free Cuba" station sponsored by the United States, or the VOA, the U.S. government's polyglot international radio and television service that was launched during the Cold War to offer an alternative to state-run media in other countries. (Al Hurra and its sibling, Radio Sawa, essentially replaced VOA Arabic.)

Though no equivalent of the Nielsen rating system exists in the Arab world, Al Hurra has been deemed an unmitigated disaster by media watchers everywhere. A 2005 Brookings Institution poll of over 3,000 Arabs found that none chose Al Hurra as their first choice for television news—and less than 4 percent of those polled named the network as a second choice even. (Interestingly, Al Jazeera was listed as number one.[5]) Al Hurra has no credibility and hence no au-

---

5. Miles, *Al Jazeera*, p. 379.

dience. The Arabs I've spoken to consider the station to be a cheap and cynical move on the part of the U.S. government. "Why does the United States think they can set up a government-run station here, when they would never do the same in America?" They've concluded that we think they are naïve or gullible—our attitude essentially conveys, "What do they know?"

They know when someone is trying to sell them something.

About a month before Al Jazeera English went live, its bureaus across the globe—in D.C., London, Doha, and Kuala Lumpur—held dry runs in preparation for the actual launch. During this period the U.S. Senate voted on the Military Commissions Act, and I appeared on the news as a military analyst after the bill passed. The legislation contained pretty much everything the president had asked for—including a controversial amendment that would deny the right of habeas corpus to Americans suspected of colluding with terrorists.

"Does this bill simply codify practices that your government was already engaged in?" I was asked. My answer was a qualified yes—that it codified practices that had been implemented by some agencies since 9/11.

"As a former soldier would you worry about how that will be perceived?"

I replied that two schools of thought prevail:

One camp says we are losing the moral high ground and this puts soldiers at risk because everyone respects the Geneva Conventions. But look back over the last 50 years and name one country the U.S. was at war with that abided by the Geneva Conventions. We know Al Qaeda doesn't. Ask Senator John McCain if they did in Vietnam. Or ask anyone who was in a Japanese POW camp in World War II. I think the boots-on-the ground perspective is, "I appreciate the Geneva accords and understand that this is how we should treat detainees." But there is no one in uniform who thinks for a second that they are going to get those rights if they are captured—not just in this war but in Afghanistan and in every previous war. The Geneva Convention seems like a high-minded ideal that only we uphold. Is it worth that to say we have the moral high ground? Or is this the kind of war where we have to get down in the mud and fight like they do?

I can't tell you how this sentiment would have been received had Al Jazeera English been broadcasting and my comments had beamed around the Arab world. But I suspect my answer might have been regarded as honest, at least, and an attempt to grapple with a real tactical and moral dilemma. Violence and conflict have shaped Arab history and it's naïve to think that viewers in the region would be appalled to hear a former military officer say, "We can fight as dirty as anyone." One of the many differences between Al Jazeera and Al Hurra is that Al Jazeera attempts to speak the truth even if the position invites controversy, and it often does.

A schizophrenic image of America exists in the Arab world. Many believe the United States represents higher values and a better way of life, which is why people line up outside U.S. embassies—even in those nations where most profess to hate the United States—and why some think the United States should adhere to international laws that other countries clearly flout. Others instead judge the United States as an arrogant and bellicose nation with imperial designs on the world, and that the Bush administration conveniently uses Al Qaeda attacks to justify the selling out of American liberties and principles.

Rather than avoid the U.S. government's contradictions—to deny that the United States supports repressive governments that are friendly to U.S. causes and interests and downgrade democratically-elected governments when Americans don't like their politics—why not confront them full on?

The United States supplies the international narrative's fodder that often serves to paint Americans as hypocritical—for example, by saying that the U.S. government supports democracy in the Western world while holding hands with Saudi Arabia and dismissing Hamas. The nation's image overseas could benefit from a PR facelift—U.S. policy and message must match. The rest of the world is not as stupid as the U.S. government must presume. Even children in the Middle East can see such obvious hypocrisy. The United States should either state that it intends to ally with nations of strategic importance, such as Saudi Arabia, while combating governments that oppose America or its allies (as in the case of Hamas, which calls for the destruction of Israel)—or the United States actually needs to support freely-elected governments like Hamas and oppose brutal, oppressive, dictatorial regimes like the ruling family of Saudi Arabia. The United States can't have it both ways. No one, for that matter, can. Not to mention that the former option pretty much outlines the diplomatic position of every successful nation state in history.

As it stands now, overseas critics of the United States take one seemingly two-faced aspect of U.S. foreign policy, and use it to undermine American credibility as a whole. I've met twelve-year-old children in the Middle East who can eloquently explain how the United States destabilized a freely-elected government in Iran in the 1950s and imposed the Shah on those people. This cultural narrative is traded on the street, passed around like baseball cards. And it's more than merely unfortunate that this worldview goes unchallenged as simplistic and naïve—it actually drives some people to blow themselves up in markets and fly airplanes into buildings.

Yet many of the United States's international critics are also drawn to the American brand that is split bi-coastally, as well as metaphorically, between Washington, D.C. and Los Angeles—the political spin of the U.S. administration and the big screen manifestation of the American dream. People criticize U.S. foreign policy, the military juggernaut, and global aspirations—all part of the U.S. brand's negative perception.

But America's image overseas is conflicted. Positive values are also associated with America, and not just the music and the movies, but the freedoms and the intangibles—the right to reinvent oneself, or to try to escape the past. This split perception might explain why, while internationally the United States's image has dipped to an all-time low, no shortage of immigrants try to come to its shores. Al Jazeera English can address those contradictions by presenting a richer picture of America.

Right now it seems that many people are left to cling to the most superficial images of the American culture. An American freelance producer I know was in Iran on business. He had hired a fixer to get him in and out of places, translate, and otherwise take the temperature of situations he found himself in. They were out in a rural area when the fixer decided it was safe to speak to him about a matter of grave import. He pulled the car over and said solemnly to the producer, "Can I ask you something very serious?"

"Of course," said the producer. "What is it?"

"Mariah Carey or Whitney Houston: who do you think is better?"

Before the invasion of Iraq in 2002, I read a survey by the International Crisis Group (ICG) in Brussels that showed that Iraqis supported the idea of a U.S. military invasion, with the caveat that the United States must get things running afterward—security had to be restored quickly, and reconstruction implemented immediately—lest Iraqi support evaporate.

The ICG poll, entitled "Voices from the Iraqi Street," was released December 4, 2002, and was based on scores of interviews with Shi'ites and Sunnis in Baghdad, Mosul, and Najaf. Those interviewed were surprisingly willing to talk; they saw the invasion as inevitable and were looking forward to the "normalcy" that would follow.

A lot of Iraqis could smell smoke in the air and were putting off major life choices—moving, getting married, going to school—until after the invasion. Many Iraqis hoped OIF would be the last in a very long line of wars fought since Saddam came to power in 1979, and that maybe peace, prosperity, and stability would prevail after U.S. combat troops set their weapons to safety. But when the Iraqis polled expected that security, electricity, and economic hope would be restored, they were talking in terms of months, not years.[6]

People love to debate whether the United States should have invaded Iraq, and what the real reasons were for going in. But to me the really important questions are: What the hell happened after U.S. troops reached Baghdad? Who allowed Bush's illusory "Mission Accomplished" to unravel?

Ironically, no one in the United States has agonized over the failure to maintain peace by rebuilding Iraq more than those in the military—and the military isn't trained to reconstruct nations beyond propping them up and securing their

---

6.   http://www.crisisgroup.org/home/index.cfm?id=2109&l=1

infrastructures. Remarkably, no U.S. governmental agency is charged with nation building as an expertise for fear that the Unites States may be viewed as imperialistic. Even more remarkably, no ad hoc organization was created to fill this void until two months before the invasion of Iraq when the administration established the Office of Reconstruction and Humanitarian Assistance (ORHA) in January 2003.

Retired Army lieutenant general Jay Garner was appointed to run ORHA, which was later absorbed by the CPA. Garner's group was tasked with getting the country going again: securing the economy, hooking up the electricity and turning the water on until a democratically elected Iraqi government could step in. In Bob Woodward's book, *State of Denial*, Garner recounts the difficulties of his post, which fell under the guidance and budget of Rumsfeld and the Department of Defense.[7]

> Garner was holding regular meetings with Rumsfeld, trying to keep him informed, get decisions and convey his growing sense of the magnitude of the task.
>
> The issue of money was omnipresent. Garner felt that almost nobody in the Bush administration thought there was going to be a big bill for the Iraq aftermath. One budget document Garner had prepared, dated February 27, 2003, showed that he had just over $27 million for his group. The numbers required for the basics of running the country were huge by comparison. He projected humanitarian assistance at over $1 billion including the next year, reconstruction at

---

7. Bob Woodward, *State of Denial: Bush at War, Part III* (Simon & Schuster, 2006), pp. 145–46.

$800 million and running the government at $10 billion—nearly $12 billion, all told. Where would it come from?

He was seeking guidance. "Hey, Mr. Secretary," Garner recalls asking Rumsfeld one day before deploying, "We've got three options. What do we want to do in reconstruction? Do you want to take everything back to where it was pre-first Gulf War? Do you want to take it back to where it was before this war? Or do you want to build all new?" The budget document also listed proposals to do a percentage of one of those periods or just repair everything. Yet no actual numbers—the important kind, with dollar signs in front of them—had been proposed.

"What do you think that will cost?" Rumsfeld inquired.

"It will cost billions of dollars," Garner answered. "Any of them will."

"Well, if you think we're spending our money on that, you're wrong," Rumsfeld said, in his most sweeping, assertive way. "We're not doing that. They're going to spend their money rebuilding their country."

Again, no one suffered (and continues to suffer) from the lack of post-invasion planning more than the U.S. troops—no one except the Iraqi people the United States intended to liberate, that is.

About a month after arriving in Baghdad, Garner and his people were abruptly relieved by Bremer and the CPA. The American media didn't seem to notice, or at least didn't say much about it. (The top news stories the next day concerned the surrender of Iraqi Deputy Prime Minister Tariq Aziz—and the release of an *Entertainment Weekly* cover featuring nude Dixie Chicks.)

If the Dallas Cowboys fired Bill Parcels and his entire coaching staff in the third game of the season, and announced a whole new staff, I guarantee the U.S. press would be all over it for weeks. Yet the administration fired the entire ORHA team. They pulled them all out and sent them packing, with hardly a blip in the U.S. media.

Envisioning the direction the United States's strategy will take in Iraq is as difficult to comprehend as what its approach there has been in the past. But it's clear that no matter what responsibility the United States assumes for repairing the damage it unleashed with its invasion, a lion's share of that effort will befall the men and women in the military. Troops will leave their families and deploy to Iraq for a long time, in one capacity or another, and the military needs to find a way to speak to that commitment and not let the events and attacks of each day define their agenda.

But often America can be an impetuous nation; this is reflected in its media, polls, and politicians. I recently addressed an audience of generals at an Air Force Base in Alabama, and the fairly freestyle event spawned an interesting conversation when a three-star general voiced his conflicted personal feelings regarding the war's difficulties.

"I feel like I can't admit wrong," he said. "I feel like I can't say something humble and introspective because if I do, and my troops are watching, and their families are watching, and the enemy is watching, it will be taken out of context. All that will be remembered is that I said something is going wrong. What happens to troop morale? To the families' morale? And for that matter, what does that do for the enemy's morale? So every time I get in front of the media I feel like I have to say everything is going great." It was an honest assessment of the dangers of mistaking a podium for a therapist's couch. The general was right to be concerned.

"What you have to do," I offered, "is have a short view and a long view in your answer. You say, 'In the short view, I regret what happened today and we're going to search in our procedures and hearts to make sure we're doing things the correct way; but in the long view, today's events will have no impact on how long we'll be here or on us straying from our mission.'"

The military has to stop banging its head against the wall, worrying about getting "the good news story" out. War is *never* a good news story. That's not what war is about inherently, so the U.S. military should stop trying to spin it. A good news story is when something good happens—stopping the violence, getting the economy going—and that kind of story *does* get out. But the good news story has to be as big as the bad news story. If you get the electricity going in a province that a reporter can't get to because it's too unsafe, and he or she reports, "The electricity is up and running, but I can't show you because I'll get my head chopped off on my way there," what part of that story do you think people are going to remember?

CHAPTER EIGHT
GOING GLOBAL: BEHIND THE SCENES AT AL JAZEERA ENGLISH

A lot of people want to know why Al Jazeera decided to launch an English language network. The answer is simple: We launched Al Jazeera English because the Emir of Qatar said to do it. He has never publicly said why he thought an English-language iteration was needed, leaving us as well as the rest of the world to speculate on his thinking, but his instincts have proven right so far. His growing media empire (which includes Arabic channels for news, sports, children's programming, C-SPAN-like public affairs coverage, and documentaries) has been a product of his hunches and vision, one that he keeps fairly private. And while conspiracy theorists inside and outside the Arab world have claimed it's a stalking horse for a political movement, or a target meant to draw fire from the more controversial Al Jazeera Arabic, all I've heard as far as our mission goes is to be as credible as possible.

Credibility is a watch word at Al Jazeera and I think it's fair to surmise that one thing the Emir wants to do is extend the credibility he has established with the Arab network to a broader, international audience. In our editorial meetings I have never heard mention of our marketing strategy, or even who our audience is meant to be. Even the competition—which for us is first and foremost the BBC World and CNN International—does not come up unless we're discussing how they are handling a story we're also covering, and how we can do it differently. The questions we ask ourselves are, "What can we add to the coverage that exists?" and especially, "Who does not have a voice in this story?" That is a question that comes up often.

If Al Jazeera English has a stated mission, it's to cover the developing world—often simply referred to as "the South"—which our competitors have too often ignored. We try to serve those underreported places and peoples while presenting aspects of western culture too often neglected in other international coverage. That's where I come in.

Though Al Jazeera English may have been discussed in theory in Doha over the last decade, the first toehold on the English language audience came with the launch of the website www.aljazeera.net/english in 2003, which was a big deal then. The satellite TV network announced its arrival when Nigel Parsons was hired as managing director of Al Jazeera English in August 2004. Nigel brought with him 30 years of experience at BBC Radio and Worldwide Television News and the announcement of his appointment was followed by a number of impressive "gets": CNN International anchor Riz Kahn was hired to host what Al Jazeera English calls the world's most interactive interview show; Sir David Frost joined with his own interview program, *Frost Over the World* (his interview with Tony Blair garnered some of Al Jazeera English's first headlines when the prime minister allowed that the Iraq war was "pretty much a disaster"); and former ABC News Nightline correspondent Dave Marash came to the D.C. Broadcast Center to anchor the news and, in his words, "seek out the areas neglected by the Western-oriented media."

As the seventh person hired by the then-nascent English-language network, I was amused when my company issued me the ID number "007." Fitting, I guess, given that some on Al Jazeera's Arabic side thought I was a spy for the U.S. government, while right-wing critics here accused me of being an agent for the Arabs.

Although the media covered Al Jazeera English's delayed launch extensively, there was certainly no subterfuge. Almost all of the American press got it wrong by speculating that the delays were because the network had not found distribution in the United States, but the truth was simply more prosaic. Our hang-ups were due entirely to the technological challenges presented by trying to hook up four international bureaus via fiber optic cable—something that went a lot more smoothly in Indonesia than here in permit-happy Washington, D.C.

As gratifying as it is to hear that we need only worry about credibility and covering stories with a fresh perspective, times arise when it would be nice to know if we are hitting our targets, even if we don't know what they are. Without the sort of Nielsen-rating data the U.S. networks rely on, I sometimes feel like we're hitting golf balls into the night. My more experienced colleagues shrug off such minor irritations, as they were lured here by the promise of editorial freedom and an opportunity to report against the grain for a while.

As of this writing, a few months after our launch, it's hard to see how our network will change going forward. Reception has been quite positive so far: the Israeli satellite system has already dropped BBC World in favor of Al Jazeera English and media critics have been encouraging as well—although the London *Times* did warn its readers that they might get depressed if they spent too much time watching us. We don't ignore such criticism, but we don't respond with stories on fuzzy puppies or twins' conventions either. Instead we try to break up the endless procession of war and poverty by mixing in stories such as the one I did about Arab actors in Hollywood fighting stereotypes. Softer spots such as that can let hard news breathe without abandoning our goal of credibility and our mission of serving those without a voice.

Before Al Jazeera English's launch, I often broke the ice in my public speaking engagements by mentioning the chilly reception I received when I called around Washington, D.C., and introduced myself to potential interviewees as a former Marine who was now shooting pilots for Al Jazeera—a joke that works because it cuts to the heart of misperceptions about the network.

But as Al Jazeera English attempted to secure U.S. distribution and I attended meetings at cable and satellite companies across the United States, their executives had little interest in me with my patriotic background and cut short my prepared answers, which attempted to overcome the U.S. misperception that we represented the ultimate in terrorist television. I quickly learned that cable companies couldn't care less about our network's content or reputation; the executives' bottom line is driven by numbers. In their experience, Americans just don't care about international news. How do they know? Their customers call and tell them what they want. And what *do* Americans request? Executives across the nation echoed the same answer: twenty-four hours of NASCAR, seven days a week.

Of course it's easier for cable executives to cite reasons like "America prefers NASCAR to Nasrullah" than it is for them to note the common misconceptions people hold about Al Jazeera. The simple truth, in the cable executives' eyes, remains that a lot of Americans don't care about international news, period. The BBC World News only recently became available in the United States on a single cable provider and

CNN International hasn't done that well. So why should Al Jazeera English be any exception?

I continue to argue, though, that the first brick in the wall of U.S. isolationism fell on 9/11, when Americans realized that the rest of the world's perceptions *do* matter. And the more Americans realize that they're involved in global political and economic relationships, the more relevant other countries and cultures with diverse outlooks will become—even if for no other reason than to understand how the differing opinions and resulting actions impact American lives.

The people in Washington, D.C., who forge our Iraq policy should be early adopters of this principle, but as Jeff Stein of the *New York Times* pointed out in his October 22, 2006, article, many still cannot distinguish between the different sects of the Muslim community. Stein spent months talking to politicians in Washington, D.C., about the war and its aftermath and always concluded with the same question: "What's the difference between a Sunni and Shiite?" His subjects included Willie Hulon, the chief of the Federal Bureau of Investigation's (FBI) new national-security branch, and Representative Jo Ann Davis, who was then heading a House intelligence subcommittee that oversaw the CIA's recruitment of Islamic spies. The answers he received were anywhere from all wrong to half-wrong—and these were people integral to our mission in a country divided along religious lines.[1]

---

1. Jeff Stein, "Can You Tell a Sunni from a Shiite?," *New York Times,* October 22, 2006, p. A21.

Al Jazeera English holds appeal for Americans who desire to become more internationalized, more in tune with the world they live in. While some Americans watch online because they feel some impulse toward enlightenment; for others it's about surviving, moving forward, and seeing their nation flourish in the twenty-first century.

Not only for its own, but for the world's sake, the United States needs to have a better understanding of the Arab world, just as the world could stand to have a better understanding of America and its complexities.

For example, people often inquire about Al Jazeera's audience in Pakistan, Afghanistan, or Iran. "There is none," I tell them, and the reason for this is simple. They don't speak Arabic in those countries because they're not Arabs. Iranians are Persians, and the language they speak is Farsi; in Afghanistan they speak Pashto, Dari, or one of many tribal tongues. Many Americans are genuinely surprised by that—they think all Muslims are Arabs. Some Americans seem to cram a lot of people into a single stereotype—people from different nations and ethnicities, who speak a host of different languages. Many also have confused notions about geography, mixing the Middle East with Central Asia or the Indian subcontinent. Pakistan is nowhere near Palestine; the two places are not in the same part of the world, but many people don't know that, and it never fails to astonish me.

Different dialects of Arabic are spoken from Morocco to Iraq and just as they share a common language, they also share a conventional wisdom about certain matters. In the United States, people rarely link the war in Iraq with the conflict in Gaza, but the Arab world believes they are the same issue. Every discussion of U.S. foreign policy in the Middle East begins and ends with Israel and Palestine.

Arabs see the Israeli military as an extension of the American military because the United States funds Israeli forces and supplies them with American military equipment. If the United States cut off all support and stopped providing Israel with weapons, the Israeli military wouldn't be what it is. At best it seems that the majority of Americans only casually consider this issue, if at all, but the Arab world is keenly aware of how our tax dollars are at work in Israel and Palestine. When people in the Arab world watch images of tanks aggressively rolling across the desert toward ill-armed civilians or, worse, children throwing rocks, it matters little to them if the tanks are plowing through the sands of Southern Iraq, or of Ramallah. The visceral power of the images catalyzes the same wellspring of emotions: Arab blood runs thick and this display of raw power is seen as an act of aggression against all Arabs.

When Americans hear that Arabs in other countries are demonstrating against the U.S. presence in Iraq, many think, "They're not Iraqi, why do they care?" The idea of Pan-Arabism and their interconnectedness is simply lost on them.

I'm not sure that many Americans are aware of how much the United States's image has suffered, and continues to suffer, in the Arab world in the wake of the latest war between Israel and Lebanon. An Army Public Affairs Officer I know often deals with Al Arabiya, the Saudi-owned news channel, and Al Jazeera's main competitor. This network is usually friendly to Americans, as most of the Arabs working at Al Arabiya are progressive and pro-Western in their outlook. "I go in there now," he told me when Israel was bombing Beirut, "and they're yelling at *me* because I'm an American. They want the bombing to stop." But many in the United States don't see the link—people may say, "Well, it's not us doing the bombing." But who is most to blame? The soldier who loads and launches a missile or the nation who funds another's army?

Early indicators support the network's gamble: the English language site, www.aljazeera.net/english, gets more American visitors than those of any other nationality and most of the interview requests from the media before the launch came from the American press as well. The media's coverage following Al Jazeera English's launch was overwhelmingly positive and celebrated the network's international outlook—one critic called Al Jazeera English "the un-CNN"—while a small camp of critics on the right reached for the usual distortions. "Jihad TV begins its hate A.M. spews update" headlined the *New*

York Post, and Katie Couric proved particularly disappoint-
ing: after her CBS news crew spent a day in Washington,
D.C., interviewing everyone in the Al Jazeera English office
except the janitor, she teased a short and biased report by
calling the station a brand extension of "Osama bin Laden's
favorite network."

In the stories I produce at Al Jazeera English, I hope to
bring aspects of the Arab experience to American viewers
while simultaneously offering an international audience more
varied and complicated glimpses of America than the one-
dimensional images they've come to expect.

Al Jazeera has always prided itself on hiring local reporters, and the English version follows suit: Nigerians report on Nigeria, and Brits cover the UK. By the same token,
I've been granted the American beat and am trying to get beyond the New York-Los Angeles-Washington, D.C., axis and
present stories from the country's fringes and heartland. So
far in my short career as an international journalist I've traveled for stories to such exotic locales as North Dakota (see
the Introduction), Texas, and Kansas, twice. I'm racking up
miles on Midwest Airlines and I've found that it's true—
Motel 6 really does keep the light on for you.

⋅⋈⋅

Al Jazeera's management wants me to shoot stories that cap-
ture the range of America's intricacies—the American

dream, warts, and all. One of my first long pieces concerns Anacostia, a historic neighborhood in Washington, D.C. (Frederick Douglass once lived there, as did Ezra Pound), which underwent a complete transformation after the Second World War. In the 1950s Anacostia's population began to shift dramatically from being roughly 90 percent white to over 90 percent African American—the population change adversely affected Anacostia's economic health as almost all of the neighborhood's services, restaurants, and stores relocated to other neighborhoods or closed. Anacostia provides a living testament to the problems of the racial divide in America. The capital of what many call the land of opportunity has a division that cuts right through its center and access to that opportunity depends on which side of the line Washingtonians call home.

Some Americans complain that my pieces play into the hands of Arab critics who believe that the United States is so mired in hypocrisy and in the denial of its own problems that Americans should not attempt to criticize any other country. My work reaches global audiences, not just Arab viewers, and my job as a journalist involves more than telling a positive story; it means finding the truth and reporting it.

If America doesn't want the rest of the world to hear that the District of Columbia is segregated and disenfranchised, that Washington, D.C., lacks representation in Congress, and that the city's incidence of AIDS is 12 times higher than the national average (roughly 1 in 20, or the same as Ethiopia), then Americans should do something about it. I live right in the heart of the problem, just a few miles from Anacostia. If I look away, am I really doing the United States a service? Americans are suffering, and my loyalty lies with what I think America should be, rather than to some protective strain in the American body politic. The story should be told, whether on Fox News or on Al Jazeera English.

But not all of my stories have a critical edge to them. I recently spent a few days at Fort Stewart, Georgia, where the U.S. Army's 1st Brigade, 3rd Infantry Division, prepared to return to Iraq—where it had already lost 317 of its soldiers—for its third year-long tour in five years. We interviewed sons and daughters seeing Daddy off to a dangerous place for such a long time that you could see, through the expressions on their young faces, their adolescent minds trying, and failing, to cope with the magnitude of the moment, while wives and mothers vowed through gritted teeth their obligatory support for President Bush and the war. You'd have to be a robot for the story to not wrench your heart. It put a sympathetic face on the soldiers that are so often demonized, or are at a minimum dehumanized, in the international press writ large. After seeing the edited piece for the first time, I paused and wondered how such a story would be received in Doha. Was it too sympathetic to the soldiers? In the end I received more positive feedback from producers and senior management in Doha about that short story than I have for any of my longer pieces that have aired to date.

Despite strong ties to the Arab world, Al Jazeera English's audience is essentially global—and mostly non-Arabic, in fact. Before the launch, I asked the network's director of distribution who its audience would be and she said, "Anyone anywhere who can speak English as a first, second, or third language." So we're talking about people in India, South America, Asia, Africa, Europe. . . . Much of Al Jazeera English's audience resides along the same routes that the English language originally took around the globe as a byproduct of British colonialism. The new network gives expatriates who have been witnesses to the Al Jazeera phenomenon, especially in the Middle East, a way of finally tapping into it.

A huge European audience follows as well, and with Al Jazeera English's four broadcast centers, news essentially follows the day around the planet.

Al Jazeera English is a network of firsts: the first global, high-definition television network, the first to split its airtime between four separate broadcast centers, and the first to stream all of its content live on the Internet, 24/7. I think originally Al Jazeera English wanted to do this to overcome any distribution problems, but now that the network is distributed to nearly 100 million homes, we're doing it because it allows us to reach an even broader, and younger, audience; it prepositions the network in the future of media distribution; and, most importantly, because it's cool.

With this twenty-first century, cutting-edge technology, Al Jazeera English wants to shake up the news agenda of the west. The BBC represents an old-world news paradigm—Anglo expats trekking around the globe and reporting back to the motherland—and CNN International is the red-headed step child of the CNN family. Al Jazeera, as a brand, is seen by many in the world as David standing up to the Goliath of the Western world.

To be at Al Jazeera during these historic times is like peering out from the epicenter of a swirling, multicultural vortex engulfing the world's population, but often even more interesting is witnessing its microscopic counterpart from within the network's office walls.

During one pilot show I co-hosted with my friend Foukara, the Washington bureau chief of Al Jazeera Arabic, we discussed the 2006 Turkish film *Valley of the Wolves*. The movie broke box-office records in Turkey, found a huge audience among Turks in Germany, and engendered considerable controversy there for its depiction of Kurds, Jews, Christians, and especially Americans. The story was inspired by a true incident in which American soldiers hooded and allegedly abused Turkish soldiers fighting in Iraq in July 2003. The film then spins off into a violent revenge fantasy that portrays U.S. soldiers attacking an Arab wedding and a Jewish-American doctor, played by Gary Busey, farming prisoners for body parts in experiments reminiscent of those conducted by the Nazis.

Foukara noted Gary Busey's A-list-actor status. "Will there be a backlash in America, seeing a big star in a film like this?" he asked me.

I laughed and said, "Gary Busey is far from being an A-list actor." The last role he landed that anyone cared about was *The Buddy Holly Story* in 1978. Since then he's made a living playing mostly villains and crazies—and occasionally mocking his own reputation by playing himself in television shows such as *Entourage*. "I don't think there's such a thing as bad publicity for Gary Busey," I said. "He would probably appreciate some backlash."

Just then Paul Gibbs, who is as British as a sterling pound, appeared from somewhere off camera and said, "You can't say that! Off-com rules, we'll get in trouble." Off-com, short for office of communications and Britain's equivalent to the United States's Federal Communications Commission (FCC), observes more stringent rules regarding slander than the United States.

"I'm not disparaging him," I said, "I'm slandering *his career!* You may think he's A-list but, believe me, in America he's off the radar." Between my Arab host, the Brit who was worried about off-com rules, and me, the funny culture-clash moment was one that no simple translation could bridge.

One of my first exposures to these sorts of internal racial and culture clashes I encountered working for Al Jazeera came not long after I was hired. Management asked a group of new employees, including me, to meet with Ahmad Maceo Eldridge Cleaver, the son of the late Black Panthers' Minister of Information Eldridge Cleaver, as part of our training. The meeting occurred during a period of time when Al Jazeera English was developing and defining its identity, and there were growing pains between it and Al Jazeera Arabic.

To facilitate international understanding, Al Jazeera hired a consultant, who was British. She divided up the room into four teams, and each engaged in exercises that were meant to break down barriers. For instance, we wrote all the stereotypes we could think of about people from the United States, the United Kingdom, the Gulf States, and Malaysia on an easel board. When we were finished we were supposed to discuss those misconceptions and laugh. My team had the United Kingdom, so we wrote things like "Bad teeth" and "Wretched food," none of which, of course, is true.

Then it was Cleaver's turn to speak. He had been born in Algeria in the seventies while his father was living in exile there, wanted by the FBI on an attempted murder charge. Cleaver had converted to Islam and written *Soul On Islam*, a nod to his father's most famous book, *Soul On Ice*, before moving to Qatar, where he had a loose affiliation with Al Jazeera. We were introduced by first name only, so I didn't realize that he had a famous family name. Noting that he was American, I asked how he had ended up in Qatar. "Well, my dad moved around a bit," he explained. He said his dad was a professor and that was why they traveled so much, and I remember thinking that it must have been an interesting life—little did I know.

Cleaver got up to give his brief. He began talking about the custom of women covering themselves head-to-toe in

Saudi Arabia. He pulled up a statistic of over 90,000 rapes reported by the FBI in the United States each year, a staggering number. By comparison, Cleaver told us how many were reported in Saudi Arabia; more like two.

The women in the room—mostly feminists and many of them seasoned enough to know firsthand the struggles of the women's movement—blew up. To them it seemed as if Cleaver were implying that rape was American women's fault for not covering themselves, all the while neglecting vital variables in the equation: the probability that a victim in Saudi Arabia will even come forward; the number of TCNs who live in Saudi Arabia that have no way of seeking justice if they are raped; how many witnesses are necessary to accuse a man of rape in a Sharia country; and the slim likelihood of Saudi Arabia publicly reporting a statistic that would be seen as disparaging of the Kingdom. He stepped on a land mine with that one.

"I can't believe you would put that up there!"

"You're just blaming the victim!"

"Don't you know that rape is always about power, not sex?"

The session was not intended to be sexual harassment training, and I'm not sure why he had been sent to talk to us. I guess they considered Cleaver to be a Muslim with one foot in America, or vice versa, and plugged in. But if Al Jazeera's executives suspected a disconnect was ripe between the cultures within Al Jazeera, they had found ample proof.

Of course management was right to try to get us talking to each other—even if one couldn't completely understand what the other was saying. A meeting of Al Jazeera's interests would look and sound like a meeting of the UN General Assembly. As Lawrence Pintak noted in the wake of the launch of the new network, "Al Jazeera English is the latest outpost in Al Jazeera's growing media empire, which includes several sports channels, a children's channel, a documentary channel, and a C-SPAN-like public affairs offering that has broken ground with programs like the first face-to-face discussion among Somalia's rival warlords." Plans for a pan-Arab newspaper, also to be called Al Jazeera, are even rumored.

These kind of moments have proved almost as common as insightful. I was visiting Al Jazeera headquarters in Doha in November 2006, just weeks before Al Jazeera English's launch, and was in a conference with a managing director, who happened to be Arab, when the head of marketing popped her head in his door to ask if he'd seen the promo online.

"It's all white," he said.

I thought he must be referring to a technical error—a newsroom with so much new technology knows its fair share of those.

"The promotional trailers," he said. "The promo we put on the web today. It shows all white people."

The most ubiquitous three-minute spot, then available online for a curious international audience, showcased a montage of reporters, anchors, producers, and cameramen, working busily before and behind the camera and, true enough, most of them were white—perhaps because the spots were representative of the first line of television professionals who hit the sands there, which was made mostly of Brits who had jumped ship from the BBC or Sky for a chance at a different market. The people making the promo probably just shot who was on hand, and, coincidentally, most of them were white. Part of it is a matter of training. The BBC has the best farm-team for international news, and many of the local reporters Al Jazeera recruited around the world don't speak English as a first language, which creates a definite challenge when one is trying to launch an English language network.

It's doubtful that an American, even one with marketing experience, would have noticed, but from the point of view of one whose job is to sell to a truly international audience, the vanilla flavor was clearly overwhelming. Al Jazeera English considers an ethnically diverse representation of employees who mirror its viewers of vital importance—lest the network resemble the BBC (and the people who colonized the Middle East) warmed over.

Al Jazeera English has made every effort to hire locals—with little-enough accent to be understood around the world—to report on the news that stems from their homelands and most directly impacts their lives.

As the network matures, it is learning from lessons such as the all-white promo and getting better at representing the cultural diversity of our audience. If you see Kamal Thayer, an Al Jazeera English reporter in Pakistan who sports a long beard and native dress, you don't need the cartouche to know you're watching Al Jazeera. His grasp of the language is flawless, and he uses 25-cent words in live reports, but I'm sure there may be people in the audience who will have to struggle with his accent. It's part of the price of being truly international.

On the day Al Jazeera English launched, it ran a live report delivered by Farai Sevenzo from Zimbabwe, where no western media had been in seven years. Sevenzo, a journalist and filmmaker based in Al Jazeera English's Harare bureau, flawlessly delivered a brave and challenging dispatch about Mugabe's failed policies: the country's 1,200 percent inflation, corruption, average life span of only 37 years, you name it. People crowded around him, fascinated by the cameras and the novelty of the situation—Zimbabwe does not allow any other media to broadcast from within its borders. And when his report was over on launch day, everyone in the Washington, D.C., studio cheered because we were proud of the coverage and what it said about Al Jazeera English: a network that could go where others could not, and that could speak truth to power. I wonder how long it will be before Zimbabwe is added to the growing list of governments that would rather ban us from the country than face critical, hard-hitting coverage—a list we take great pride in.

On the verge of Al Jazeera's expansion from a regional phenomenon to a global one, the network paused for a ceremony commemorating the tenth anniversary of Al Jazeera

Arabic's launch in November 2006. I happened to be in Doha at the time.

On the evening of November 1 I left the newsroom in Doha and walked across the street to the outside area, next to Al Jazeera's headquarters and where the ceremonies were to be held. I expected to meet my friend Omar Il Assawi there but ended up strolling around until I wandered into a foyer that housed a museum-style exhibit dedicated to the decade of Al Jazeera. Through glass doors you could see The Wall of Freedom outside—a 55-foot-tall memorial commemorating 630 journalists from around the world who had died or disappeared in the line of duty—that was being dedicated as part of the evening's ceremonies. While the names, etched on raised rectangles on a black marble wall, represented international journalists of every stripe, a separate exhibit for Al Jazeera's own was in this foyer. There behind glass was the helmet and flak jacket that did not save the life of Al Jazeera correspondent Ayyoub when U.S. forces bombed Al Jazeera's Baghdad bureau in the early weeks of the war. Sami Al Hajj, a freelance cameraman who was working for Al Jazeera when he was captured by U.S. troops in December 2001 on suspicion of working with Al Qaeda, was also represented. At this writing, almost five years after the fact, he is still being held at Guantanamo Bay even though no evidence of the charges against him has been presented. As Nicholas Kristof wrote in a *New York Times* editorial in October 2006, "There is no public evidence that Sami al-Hajj committed any crime other than journalism for a television network the Bush administration doesn't like."[2] As I stood there among the displays to its fallen or captured heroes, I couldn't help but think that this was the building Bush and Blair had joked about bombing. (The FBI memorializes their fallen agents with similar displays in the foyers of agency buildings. Ironically, they call them walls of martyrs.)

Workers were still running around getting ready for the celebration. The ceremonies themselves were to take place outside in the desert air. On a raised platform was a lectern for the evening's speakers along with three giant video screens.

The ceremony started at seven. We headed for our seats, passing a long table groaning with food and spectacular centerpieces, including an ice sculpture of an elaborate Middle Eastern teapot, tall and ornate. A teapot is hot; I kept thinking in a fixated jet-lagged mindset, and laughed to myself. It was fall in Doha, which means it was a muggy 95 degrees. A frozen teapot in the warm desert air: contradictions within contradictions.

A couple thousand formally dressed people were easily present and awaited the Emir's arrival. My mind kept wandering back to the teapot; I couldn't help thinking while we waited that time was passing and that it must be melting. Finally, the Emir swept in with an entourage of a couple dozen

---

2. "Sami's Shame, and Ours," *New York Times*, October 17, 2006.

people. He went to the front of the crowd, sat in a plush chair, and was immediately served tea.

The program began with both male and female presenters in formal dress, reading from cards in Arabic. A video montage from the last ten years was shown on the three fifty-foot screens—including intifada scenes, the Twin Towers falling in 2001, the invasion of Afghanistan, and the Iraq war. The montage included footage of Donald Rumsfeld at Pace University saying, "If you have people like Al Jazeera pounding people in the region with things that are not true then it is not easy. We know it has a pattern of playing propaganda over and over again."

A short documentary about the history of the network was followed by several speeches, all in Arabic. Tayseer Al-louni, an Al Jazeera reporter under house arrest in Spain for suspected Al Qaeda ties, spoke to the crowd from the video monitors. Then suddenly we were in the Piacenza Theater in Northern Italy where the Italian Philharmonic Orchestra and Choral Group was performing an original symphony. The piece, entitled "Sharq" ("The East"), was by the Lebanese composer Marcel Khalife and had been commissioned by the network expressly for the occasion. While we listened and watched in Doha, the Italian Philharmonic played—and played, for ten, twenty, thirty minutes. The whole show was being broadcast live on Al Jazeera.

I was getting ready to call it a night and go home, when Ibrahim Helal, a managing director, ran toward me and a group of reporters and shouted, "Get to the news room, he's coming!" We all rushed to newsroom, and the Emir entered with his entourage—his wife, their handlers, and bodyguards—along with Khanfar, Nigel Parsons, the managing director of Al Jazeera English, Helal, and others. I was twenty feet from the Emir when I realized I had no idea what the protocol is: do I presume to speak to him? Wait to be introduced? In that world he is the ultimate power and I couldn't do anything. I was standing there, stuck in the middle of the newsroom. Even though I had spent the last year with Arabs from the network and had studied the history and culture of Qatar, I had no idea how to act or react in that situation. Talk about a cultural disconnect.

Helal was talking with the Emir and pointing at me. I could read his lips saying that I had been a Marine and that I now worked for Al Jazeera English. Suddenly the Emir looked at me, smiled, waved and said, "Hello." I had no idea how to respond. So I half waved and stood there awkwardly holding the palm of my hand toward him and offered a tentative "Hello." Then I turned tail and walked briskly away to where a group of anchors were watching.

Then Helal guided the Emir to where I had retreated and introduced me to him. Helal said, "Tell him about the piece you are working on." I started babbling about the program I was filming, *Spin*, going on about political disinformation and the place of veracity in public affairs, but how this was also a personal story because of my history. Using archival footage of lies and half-truths that had been sold to the American people to justify previous U.S. mili-

tary interventions, and borrowing from the historical reporting style of Norman Solomon, *Spin* was unique in that
it featured the person reporting the story in its indictment:
there was footage of me before the invasion of Iraq telling
a reporter from Fox News about the atrocities of Saddam
and the people's need for liberation, as well as the scenes
from *Control Room* where I espoused the party line. I explained that *Spin* would soon be my first special on Al
Jazeera English and one that forged a personal bridge between my past and my current job as a journalist. After a
minute or so I finally stopped talking. The Emir looked at
me for an awkwardly long time and then he walked on
without saying a word.

My first thought was that I had misread the entire situation. Maybe because the Emir is a strong American ally, he
was uninterested in hearing anything inherently critical
about the U.S.'s martial intentions. After all, if the Emir is
taking a risk in the Middle East by allowing Al Jazeera to
anger some of Qatar's neighbors, he does so with the insur-
ance of having one of the largest U.S. military installations in
the region on his land. I was beginning to suspect that as
much as I thought I knew about Al Jazeera and my place in it,
I was really like an explorer in a new world, taking my first
steps, learning my first words. I needed someone to translate
the speeches I had heard that evening. Maybe this meeting
needed an interpreter as well.

Then I met one of the network's anchors, the Greek journalist Elizabeth Fillipouli. With 14 years of experience as an

anchor and interviewer at the Hellenic Broadcasting Corporation, Fillipouli had been like the Couric of Greece. She had joined Al Jazeera English, she told me, to reach an international audience.

I told her of my curious meeting with the Emir. "I didn't know the protocol for talking to him," I was saying when she grabbed my wrist and said, "He's over there; let's ask him for a picture." In the photo, the light is rather orange, the newsroom in the background looks like it could be the flight deck of the Starship Enterprise in Star Trek. A glare traces the makeup of the striking Fillipouli. I have a broad smile on my face. The Emir of Qatar, like a lion accustomed to unquestioned power, patiently allows the moment to be captured forever.

POSTSCRIPT
BUILDING THE BRIDGE

L ast fall, I spoke to a group of general officers at Maxwell Air Force Base in Alabama. I'll admit I was nervous about this particular engagement. It's one thing to lecture a bunch of cadets at West Point; they are young and haven't yet held the rank I did when I left the Marine Corps. But the audience at Maxwell promised to be a little different: the roughly two-dozen men in attendance were mostly either two- or three-star generals, drawn from all branches of the military. Not many people bear this rank, and these were the best of the best, generals slated to assume joint commands. If an officer is particularly ambitious, he or she seeks a joint command, one that combines all the services. These generals had been selected for the most competitive commanding general spots in the armed forces.

Heading into this conference I was concerned about running into a general hearing a personal story about being burned by an Al Jazeera reporter. Most audiences I speak to don't know anything about Al Jazeera; they haven't engaged with the network in any capacity. But I knew the odds favored the possibility that these generals had served in the Middle East, and they might have some firsthand encounter with a reporter for which they would hold me accountable. Every network has ambitious reporters that often leave a trail of bitter subjects, and my network is no different in this regard.

I'd experienced this once before at the Annual Dinner of the Radio & Television Correspondents' Association on March 29, 2006, when I spoke with Marine Lieutenant General James Mattis. I introduced myself as a former Marine captain who now works for Al Jazeera, and that set him off. "Those sons of bitches said I used white phosphorous in Fallujah and I never did!" he snarled. Before I could get the details of what he was talking about, so that I might track down the ground truth, he stormed off. I remember thinking: *That didn't go so well.*

As I prepared for the conference with a couple dozen more potentially cantankerous generals who were not accustomed to being told anything by anyone, I hoped my fortune would be different.

As any good Marine who is concerned about an ambush would do, I did some reconnaissance before I left for the engagement. I called the colonel who was helping coordinate the course to see what I could possibly bring to the table.

I got a good sense from him what sort of territory I was headed into. In discussing his thoughts about the military's relationship with the media, he said, "Well, I think Bill Keller, the editor of the *New York Times*, should be put in jail for leaking classified information. And I believe that CNN is traitorous. . . ." *Boy*, I thought, *you're going to love the guy from Al Jazeera.*

On the flight down I outlined my remarks. I decided to build on the generals' experiences rather than avoid them. Pointing out that Qatar is a key American ally, for instance, would resonate with anyone who had served in the Middle East. Considering that the Al Udeid Air Base is of undeniable strategic importance, I hoped they could at least admit that Al Jazeera, funded by the same government and located just across town from the air base, might not be that bad.

The panel's first speaker was classified and those of us not in the military and without clearance waited outside. The second general had overseen strategic communications in Baghdad during the first national elections. The panel evolved into a forum—where the audience would interrupt the guest speaker to ask questions or take issue with what was being said. One general, a retired three-star, seemed to run the show by throwing out tough questions to the speaker on behalf of the participants. I remember him kibitzing with the former strategic communications general about someone who had been picked for an important task: "You can't send a young one-star out to do that kind of job." That told me something about the mentality of these guys. It takes twenty-odd years of an absolutely stellar career to get one star. If they thought of one-stars as neophytes, what were they going to think of a former captain telling them how it really is with Al Jazeera?

I was preceded on stage by two other reporters: Jonathan Karl, who covers the State Department and the Pentagon for ABC, and William Arkin, a columnist for *Washington Post.com*, who specializes in national and homeland security. Arkin, who spoke just before me, was frankly hostile. He stood up in front of them and said things I've never heard anyone say to a general. He told them that they were naïve, that they couldn't speak English, and that they had failed in Iraq. When I got up there I said, "Thanks to Bill Arkin for clearing the way for me. I was worried about being the Al Jazeera guy, but what could I say that could be any worse than that?" The faintest hint of a smile spread across the assembly.

I delivered my joke about shooting pilots for Al Jazeera, which got the laugh I needed, and then moved on to my three-part presentation. The first part concerned Al Jazeera: what it is and what it is not (i.e., it's not the incendiary website Al Jazeera.com, it's not the beheading network, and it's not affiliated with Al Qaeda). I reminded them of the United

States's ally, Qatar, of our airbase and CentCom headquarters there, and how the Qatari government funds Al Jazeera in much the same manner the United Kingdom funds the BBC. Next I talked about Al Jazeera English, its expected launch, and what we hoped it would be.

Finally, as a guy who had been in both their world and the Arab media, I gave them a three-part recommendation: strategic, tactical, and intellectual. My strategic advice concerned enabling progressive reporters at Al Jazeera, finding open-minded correspondents, and giving them the same kind of access they would give a reporter from Fox News. "You'll be helping them get through to the people they answer to," I said. "You will offer your side of the story to their editorial meetings. It's a way of getting out stories you want but with a credibility that your military spokesperson will never have."

Then I presented my tactical advice. I told them the hypothetical story about the Marine squad that returned fire on some insurgents inside a mosque, the runaround the Al Jazeera reporter received from the military, and how the network ended up going with the insurgents' version of events. "The tactical error became a strategic mistake," I said, "and here's what I recommend you do to avoid that mistake in the future: make 'public affairs' part of your combat training. Right now you do combat training—marksmanship, hand-to-hand combat, patrolling techniques—say, Monday through Thursday. Then on Friday, as sort of an afterthought, you add public affairs to the leftovers. By lumping it in with the admin paperwork and filling out wills with the legal department, you have already indicated to your troops that it's not that important, certainly not a matter of life or death.

"Next, you need to trust your lower level troops to speak to the press. A friend of mine is a commander in the Navy SEALs, who says, 'There's no way I'm going to let my guys speak to the press because there is no way to tell what they're going to say!' Okay, so you don't trust all of them. But one person in that squad must be designated as spokesperson." A basic squad consists of thirteen people: three fire teams of four marines each and then a squad leader. Each one of these soldiers has collateral duties, such as a machine-gunner or a fire-team leader. I told these generals, "If you can trust these young men and women to walk through a village with little supervision, while carrying a grenade launcher and a machine gun, then you can trust one of them to tell the reporters on the scene how a battle went down. You can trust one of them to think on his or her feet and give a reporter the right public affairs officer to call for any further information they might need. That will save lives, theirs and possibly others, just by giving out the right information at the scene."

Third, I called for an intellectual shift regarding their relationship to the Arab media. With Al Jazeera, I argued, Qatar was bringing the media age to the Middle East and beyond in much the same way the British exported the English language in the time of Queen Victoria. I quoted a famous retired Marine general named Walter Boomer, who has a good reputation for being great with the press, and who said after Desert Storm, "The media are like rain on the battlefield. We have to know how to operate with them around us all the time. If it rains you don't stop fighting; you know how to operate and accomplish your mission no matter what the weather." I took his analogy one step further. "The media have *become* a battlefield," I argued, "in the larger global war on terror. You need to ask yourself if you're even on that battlefield and if you're ready to engage in the conflict."

My speech garnered a tremendous response. The generals approached me afterward and shook my hand, saying things like, "I didn't know that Al Jazeera had such a global reach." Then a Marine general pulled me aside. "I'm a reservist on active duty," he said. "I'm in charge of training all reserve Marines who are going to Iraq. They have to go through my desert training program at Twentynine Palms, California, before they ship out. I'm going to go back and change the training based on your advice."

I couldn't have made that change in the Marine Corps had I wanted to, but I may have done it by joining Al Jazeera English. It's hard to explain how good that felt. I had been nervous to go in front of these generals, even though I consider it part of my job to draw fire as the guy from "Terrorist TV."

But I have an important message to carry as well, one that could actually make a difference. Someone got it, and this time he was someone who could do something with it. These generals listened to me, not just because I was a former Marine, but also because I understood the Arab media. I am that bridge I had always imagined I could be, without worrying about the lanes.

INDEX

INDEX

ABOUT THE AUTHOR

JOSH RUSHING works for Al Jazeera English as a military and current affairs correspondent. While providing news packages and insight on military issues, the Texas native also shoots thought-provoking stand-alone specials and long-form documentaries. A former U.S. Marine captain with 15 years of service, Josh served as a spokesperson at Central Command during Operation Iraqi Freedom. Unbeknownst to him the documentary film, *Control Room*, captured his efforts to communicate the American message on Al Jazeera. Josh speaks to universities and organizations across America and around the world. He has been featured in *GQ*, *Fast Company* magazine, *Time Magazine*, and *USA Today*, and has appeared on *The Today Show*, *Anderson Cooper 360*, and *The O'Reilly Factor*. Josh lives in Washington, D.C, with his wife and two sons. Please visit www.JoshRushing.com.

SEAN ELDER's writing has appeared in Salon.com, *Details*, *New York* magazine, *The New York Times Magazine*, *National Geographic*, and many other publications. He teaches writing at Eugene Lang College, New School University and lives in Brooklyn.